# THE COURAGE TO CHANGE

*Empowering Your Life From the Inside Out*

Marilyn Gustin

D0109514

**LIGUORI**
PUBLICATIONS

One Liguori Drive
Liguori, MO 63057-9999
(314) 464-2500

**Library of Congress Cataloging-in-Publication Data**

Gustin, Marilyn N. (Marilyn Norquist)
    The courage to change : empowering your life from the
inside out / by Marilyn Gustin.
            p.    cm.
        ISBN 0-89243-867-3
        1. Self-efficacy—Religious aspects—Christianity. 2. Change
(Psychology)—Religious aspects—Christianity.  3. Christian life.
4. Meditation.    I. Title.
BV4598.236.G87    1996                                95-42792
248.4—dc20

Copyright © 1996, Marilyn Gustin
Printed in the United States of America
95 96 97 98 99   5 4 3 2 1

Scriptural citations are taken from the *New Revised Standard Version
Bible.* Copyright © 1989 by the Division of Christian Education of
the National Council of the Churches of Christ in the United States
of America. Used with permission.

# INTRODUCTION

Much has been said and written in the last ten years about women's power to create their own lives. When I asked a large number of women how they tried to do that, they talked about the primary capacity they had discovered within themselves: the capacity to make their own choices. Asked for examples, without exception they spoke of choices about their circumstances. No one spontaneously mentioned their power to choose about themselves, to determine their own inner experiences.

Yet our power of choice in our mental, emotional, and spiritual lives is the mightiest capacity we have. Even though we have seldom heard about it and perhaps tried it out even less, we *can* choose the quality of our inner experience. That choice will change everything else.

There is a universal principle involved here. It is actually a basic spiritual understanding too often lost to many ordinary women in today's world. That essential law is this: The Inner Determines the Outer.

This law means that what we are inside determines what happens in our external world—our homes, our jobs, our creativity, our friendships, our churches, our communities.

As long as we continue to focus on the external situations in our lives, the quality of our experiences will stay largely the same. If we want our lives to have a new and more beautiful quality (and who doesn't?), we can go after it by making new choices about our emotions, our attitudes, and our habitual thoughts. In that arena, we are far more powerful than we know. Experiments can teach us just how powerful we are—and then we're off to a brand new experience of our life.

We may stay in the same home, family, church, town, and job. When the quality of our inner experience becomes different, the quality of our outside experience will be altered. There is no "maybe" about this. It is as universal a law as gravity.

Why haven't we known about this before now? Well, many have. But it is often not popularized because it depends on a fundamental willingness: the willingness to take responsibility for the quality of one's own experience.

Responsibility does not mean blame. Not at all. It means the ability to respond. In looking toward inner choices and inner changes, we take up an often-ignored ability to choose our responses to everything and everyone. If we do that, and if we follow up by making clear choices about what qualities we want to experience, we can totally alter the quality of our life.

Too many women still have the feeling that they are stuck by forces beyond their control. Their husbands, their children, economic strains, the rules of society or religion—all kinds of ordinary women's experiences lead to a feeling of helplessness. When we live from this feeling, we are never quite happy and far from fulfilled. When we live from this feeling, we also tend to blame everyone and everything *except ourselves* for our condition. Many of us have been taught a skewed kind of religion that suggests that women *should* let their families, spouses, and communities determine the nature of their lives. It's called self-sacrifice, and it is deadly to the human spirit.

Sacrifice means "to make holy." It does not mean to throw away our God-given powers. It does not mean to capitulate to every need of every person around us. It does not mean that we are expected by God to become doormats—nice ones, but doormats just the same.

To sacrifice means to make ourselves holy by offering ourselves to God in love and freedom. We are unable (to say nothing of unwilling) to do this if we have not discovered that we have something real and valuable and strong to offer to God. An essential ingredient in that discovery is the recognition of our human capacity to choose our own attitudes and values and to allow our choices to flow into actions.

That's the reason for this book. I have experimented and observed the power of choice over inner conditions quite deliberately for well over a dozen years. I have learned. This book shares my learning.

I wish to offer each reader one caution. This book's suggestions are not intended primarily for people with major trauma in their background. Hundreds of thousands of ordinary women have a certain number of problems and challenges in their background, but actually function quite well in their daily lives. Many, many still feel trapped and helpless, even without major trauma. Some may wonder why they are always vaguely unhappy when their lives really "haven't been *that* bad."

If you have had major trauma, you may not be quite ready for these suggestions. You may need some professional guidance. If you do, get it! Then you can get on with your own life.

If you are a woman who just wants your life-quality to improve without having to create a major revolution in home and family relationships or in other circumstances, then this book is for you. Its message is simple to say, even though the experience cannot be created overnight. Its message is this:

*You are not helpless.*
*You are a person of great power.*
*Your personal power is your power to choose your own inner qualities.*

I assure you, it is a fascinating voyage, this trip into the inner world where you are in charge. I invite you, I urge you, to jump at the possibility. This book will get you started—if you *do* inside yourself what is offered here. It has worked for me and for thousands who have proven these principles for themselves. It will work for you.

# CONTENTS

# CHAPTER ONE

# USE YOUR POWER
# TO CHOOSE

*The most common despair is to be in despair*
*of not choosing, or willing, to be oneself.*
SØREN KIERKEGAARD

*Knowing how to choose is one of heaven's greatest gifts.*
BALTASAR GRACIÁN

Know how to choose. Most things in life depend on it. You need good taste and an upright judgment; intelligence and application are not enough. There is no perfection without discernment and selection. Two talents are involved: choosing and choosing the best.

There are many people with a fertile, subtle intelligence, rigorous judgment, both diligent and well informed, who are lost when they have to choose. They always choose the worst, as though they wanted to demonstrate their skill at doing so.

"Have you ever been victimized?" When I ask that question of an audience, there is a resounding *yes*! Almost no voice out there is missing. Everyone has experienced the victimized feeling. Some of us have adopted it permanently.

To each of us, things happen which we do not seem to choose and which we do not like. They come from outside ourselves; they are due to circumstances over which we have "no control." They result from a decision by another person, from a change at work, from illness or an accident, from a loss or a death or a natural catastrophe. And we cannot change what has happened. We cannot make another person love us again; we cannot *not* have the accident we had or call someone back from death. These things bring our life to a sudden halt; it cannot go on in the way it always did before. We suddenly feel our limitations.

"Victimizing" events usually leave us feeling helpless. We feel that we have, after all, nothing to say about what happens to us. We may feel trapped. We may feel betrayed or abandoned. Our feelings may erupt in anger, a pointless lashing out at other people or at God. Or we may experience a kind of despair and give ourselves over to helplessness. We may become depressed and begin to sleep away a life that has lost its flavor or begin to eat almost nothing. At one time or another, I have felt all of these emotions and consider them perfectly natural. Thank goodness they usually don't come all at once!

People react differently to these experiences of helplessness. Some of us scrabble as hard as we can merely to cope; we don't try to "respond," only to keep our footing. Others get very angry and try to resist or change the unchangeable. Still others give up and mope, saying, "There's nothing I can do anyway." They probably add, "Poor me!"

Each of these reactions has at sometime been my own. I

found that none of them worked very well. In fact, I felt much worse after a few days of indulging in such feelings, and they didn't seem to make anything else better either. The circumstances didn't change; everything seemed to slide a little further downhill.

If this happens often enough, we can become convinced that we really are victims and can do nothing about the quality of our experience. Then, of course, we habitually blame everything outside ourselves for the mess within us. We go around saying to ourselves and others, "Well, I had a dysfunctional family." Or, "Those kids make me feel so inadequate." Or, "The Church makes me feel so guilty." Or, "God took him away and now I'll feel lonely forever." In one way or another we express the conviction: "Somebody did it to me. I am a victim. There is nothing I can do about it." And with this attitude, we crawl into a deep pit and take up residence there.

If this description brings back familiar feelings, take a moment to examine them. Our feelings affect us and need to be dealt with, but they are often not the best indicator of the truth of a situation. Let's reflect now together.

When God made us, we were given a unique and wonderful power that most of us take for granted. Though we may not use this power much, or use it so automatically that we hardly notice it, nevertheless it is God-given. If this power has been weakened by disuse or misdirected, we can reclaim and develop it. It is this power that can change our lives, if we use it deliberately. It is *the power to choose.*

The power to choose is not the power to determine everything that happens to us. Some circumstances are indeed beyond its reach, although I suspect these are fewer than we assume. We cannot always choose events. But we can *always* choose our own attitude toward all events, toward all people, toward all experiences, toward unknown mysteries, and even toward God.

This fact about humans has been demonstrated in the most extreme situations. In concentration camps, some people were filled with hatred for their persecutors, while others in the same camp prayed with compassion for their captors. In desperation, some did everything and anything to ensure their own survival, while others shared the meager supplies they had. Some found meaning in their experience; others found only meaningless horror. Their external circumstances were the same. Their inner situation, their own inner choices, differed. Those choices created the *quality* of their experience. If people in such hells can choose their attitudes, surely we can too. We need only to practice.

Every adult woman makes this basic choice: to be a victim or to take responsibility for the quality of her own life. We decide either by default, in which case we are choosing to be victims, or we can decide deliberately. If we choose deliberately, we probably will choose to be responsible. Only a few women enjoy feeling helpless. When the alternatives are clear, most of us will choose to be responsible, because the results are infinitely better.

When I choose responsibility, I enjoy life more. I can make mistakes and not be crushed. I feel solid about myself, about my relationships. Even my relationship with God is better.

To "accept responsibility" or to "be responsible" is not the same thing as accepting blame or believing that "it's my fault." Accepting responsibility does not increase one's guilt. Responsibility literally means "the ability to respond." To respond is not the same as to react. Reaction is automatic. In reaction, we usually revert to childish patterns. Responsibility is the attitude that says, "Well, these are the situations I'm in. How do I wish to respond to them? What feelings and actions do I wish to put into the circumstances? How can I express and attract the quality I desire to experience now, in this situation?"

I myself learned deliberate choice of responsibility only after I found myself in an extremely painful corner. Only later did I realize that the experience put an end to my useless quest for a magician or a charming rescuer to fix my life.

The corner? I was abandoned and betrayed by a person to whom I had been profoundly committed.

I'd like to say that I bravely took stock of the situation, made all the right choices, and went on with my life. But I didn't. I felt angry. I felt very frightened. I felt that the foundation I'd really depended on was gone and that I might fly to pieces for good. I cried a lot. I slept a lot. I prayed—after a fashion. It mostly sounded like "Help!" and "How could you?" and "Why aren't you doing something?" I felt duped and foolish and exposed. I felt victimized and abused. More accurately, I felt totally helpless.

Still, nagging me beneath all this emotion was the recognition that nothing would change the other person's decisions—least of all, me. Then one day my anger found new words: "I'll be darned if I'm going to let *you* run my life! I will not be controlled by this. I will *not* be a victim! *I* will determine the quality of my life!"

Then, I guess, my garbled prayers were answered. I had a special moment of insight. I saw that, although I was spewing anger, the determination to create the quality of my own life came from a deeper place within me. I had heard that people could create their own attitudes. Now would come the practical test. Amid all the turmoil, could I choose?

I looked for someone who could tell me how to do it, but I couldn't find anyone—maybe I just asked the wrong people. I stumbled around a lot trying to find out how to be responsible, how to make my life-quality my own. Since then I've reflected a lot on that awful experience (and other lesser ones). I've also practiced responsibility more and more.

Here are the steps that help me; I hope you will find them useful as well.

- *Decide to be honest with yourself about whatever is going on inside you.* You can only choose a new attitude if you are pretty clear about how you already feel. Do not *evaluate* your inner feeling-state too quickly. Evaluation can muddy your perception. What is needed is to see clearly *what* is going on inside. You can never change anything you do not see. So the honesty needed here is the willingness to see without any distortion.

  What is going on? Just look at whatever it is. Give names to your feelings. If looking inside triggers pain or tears or regrets, notice them all. Allow them to be there. Be honest about their presence and study how they behave inside you. Which feeling seems to trigger which? How do the feelings affect each other? What actions do they seem to promote? Can you find the feelings in your body? Where? Questions like these, addressed to yourself, will help you learn what your present attitudes are.

- *Accept the circumstances as fact.* These realities do not have to be approved of, liked, or wanted. It is important to recognize that they are there and they may not change. I was helped by the definite knowledge that these circumstances would not change. I went on crying over them, but I accepted the "no hope" situation as a fact. With that acceptance comes a certain freedom—knowing exactly where you stand. The capacity to choose is strengthened by that knowledge.

  If you find yourself in pain, acknowledge it, but don't

wallow in it. For once, without denial of the hurt, be brave and learn to endure it. If you must express your pain, find an appropriate way that won't make your situation worse. If your pain seems overwhelming, talk to a professional or a trusted friend. But no matter how you choose to respond to this pain, be willing to bear it with courage as long as it remains. Pain so borne can be purifying and strengthening. Don't waste it!

- *Look for your bottom-line feeling.* That's the feeling that remains yours in spite of everything. I had loved this person before. Do I still love? It nearly killed me—or so I thought—to feel love underneath all the other junk, but it was there. It was my bottom-line feeling.

- *Explore the ways your bottom-line feeling can bring you closer to God.* There is no formula for this. I believe, however, that everyone's bottom-line feeling is good. To discover this deep feeling, ask yourself over and over: "I see this obvious feeling. What is beneath it?" And then when you find the next layer, what is beneath that? Keep going until you know you are at the deepest, truest feeling you have. If you are unable to do this at one sitting, then allow the question to remain open until the next layer reveals itself—for it will.

  All of us, no matter how deep we must dig, will find something lovely at bottom: that we love or want love, that we are kind or want kindness, that we are healthy or want health, that we are good and long for goodness. Our own disregard of these basics may well have brought trouble. Anything good in us will increase and multiply if we attend to it and act on it. That goodness is of God. It can lead us toward God.

- *Pray about the bottom-line feeling.* Let it lead you to explore yourself in the presence of God. In focusing on love in my prayer, I soon saw that my love and commitment had not been so pure. Love was mixed with need—and fantasy and wishes too. In some hidden way I had surrendered myself to someone else, hoping that I would be relieved of the necessity of living my own life. In other words, unknown to myself, I had mixed love with non-responsibility. Now I could see, slowly and with considerable embarrassment, that much of my pain was fear of being truly responsible. I found that choosing to focus on love and remain loving strengthened me, when nothing else was mixed up in it. All good bottom-line feelings bring such strength.

- *Choose to recall and focus on the positive feeling as often as you can and for as long as you can.* Remind yourself that you can choose that feeling. You are not helpless in your own inner life. You can be responsible for its quality in every circumstance. Do it now—at this moment...and this moment...and this moment.

- *Be grateful and express your gratitude.* In the beginning, you may be grateful only for survival! But with time, you can become grateful for insight, for the power to choose, for the option to be responsible. You will find yourself grateful for the presence and help of God. One day you will even be grateful for the "circumstances beyond control" that halted you in your tracks, that helped you to stop being a victim and to move toward creating the quality of life you desire under God.

Prayer and gratitude bring a far more valuable gift than simply assistance with a present difficulty. They bring us closer and closer to God. Sometimes that's why a difficulty is allowed into our lives: so we will pray more and discover more gratitude, so that we will be more intimate with the Lord. Our relationship with God is all that matters in the end. God is more important than any situation or any of our emotions. And God does not care *how* we come to him. He cares that we come, so he can shower us with all of his love.

The results of practicing the choice of responsibility may come quite suddenly. Some of us are simply ripe for it. Or the results may take time to appear. When anyone accepts full responsibility for his or her life, before God, things do change. Feelings change. Needs are filled differently and more effectively. Circumstances change too. New kinds of daily choices are made, and they in turn affect the larger situation.

The results I've noticed can be summed up as an awareness of personal power. That does not mean power *over* anyone else. It does not mean that everything always goes the way I wish it. It does mean I am aware of the capacity for beautiful living that God has implanted in me—and in you!

Personal power means I can find meaning and growth possibilities in every situation. Personal power means I know that not only can I cope, but I can make the wonderful happen in my life. Personal power means that no one victimizes me. I am aware that I may have somehow contributed to the painful occurrences in my life, even if only by what I have not done. I accept that. Since I accept it, I can much more easily choose the attitude that will give to my whole life a positive, enjoyable quality.

All this does not imply that my emotions never vary! The nasty feelings come sometimes, bring their chaos, and pass again. The difference is that now I know that I need not be the victim of my own feelings.

After all, a single day's observation will show unmistakably that emotions are a lot like the weather—they change at the slightest provocation. They come, sometimes like strong storms, and they also leave when they are spent or when our attention shifts or when we choose to pursue new attitudes. Emotions are not ultimate. They are a powerful part of our make-up, but they are transient. They are not as strong as the power of choice God gave me. So even when emotions catch me unawares, I know they are not here to stay.

Something much firmer *is* here to stay: I choose never to be a victim. I choose to be responsible for the quality of my life. I choose to create the quality of life that I most deeply desire. *That* is empowering.

More important even than this wonderful empowerment is a new realization of God's power. When we choose a positive attitude, when we choose to bear difficulties courageously, we allow our hearts to open. An open heart finds God. An open heart discovers in experience that God is on our side. God wants to help. God always does help, if we are not clinging to an inferior attitude that prevents us from receiving this help. When we wish to be responsible, God is always right in our heart, ready to back us with his own infinite power.

## Suggestions for Prayer

Pray about responsibility in your own words. You may consider these suggestions:

- leveling with God about your situation: circumstances, feelings, pains, desires;
- asking for God's guidance toward responsibility;
- telling God your intention to create a lovely life even in

these circumstances and asking for God's blessings on your efforts;

- giving all the results over to God;
- thanking God.

Or you may find it easier to begin with these words:

*Gracious God, thank you for loving me, even though right now it's hard to see what your love means. I feel so helpless—not just now but in most of my life. I feel trapped and uncertain. It hurts a lot. Sometimes I get very scared and angry, even at you. I want my life to be beautiful. I'm willing to do my part to make it beautiful. Please help and guide me. Show me how I can improve my choices. Please bless my efforts, for without your blessing it will all be futile.*

*I offer all this to you. It's all I can offer right now. I offer you, too, whatever happens as my choices get to be more responsible. Thanks for understanding and thanks for giving me the power to choose the quality of my life.*

## Scripture Suggestions

Pondering these verses may help:

*Deuteronomy 30:19-20*
I call heaven and earth to witness against you today that I have set before you life and death, blessings and curses. Choose life so that you and your descendants may live, loving the LORD your God, obeying him, and holding fast to him; for that means life to you and length of days, so that you may live in the land that the LORD swore to give to your ancestors, to Abraham, to Isaac, and to Jacob.

*Proverbs 20:22*
Do not say, "I will repay evil";
   wait for the LORD, and he will help you.

*1 Corinthians 2:9-10*
But, as it is written,
"What no eye has seen, nor ear heard,
   nor the human heart conceived,
what God has prepared for those who love him"—
these things God has revealed to us through the Spirit;
for the Spirit searches everything, even the depths of God.

Here are some additional Scriptures for further reflection:

*Psalm 8:4-9*        *Luke 16:1-8*        *John 14:1-27*

## For Reflection

These questions may get you started on the process of self-assessment described in this chapter:

- Do I really believe that circumstances result from my attitudes? If yes, then what are some examples in my own life? If no, why not?
- When have I felt the most victimized? How did I respond to those circumstances and the feelings that went with them? What could I do if that happened today?
- Am I feeling victimized now? By what or whom? What are the emotions I am feeling? What is my bottom-line feeling? What do I wish to choose?
- In what areas of my life am I responsible already? In what areas can I choose to become more responsible?

$\mathcal{C}$HAPTER $\mathcal{T}$WO

# DON'T WASTE
# YOUR PAIN

*Pain is the root of knowledge.*
SIMONE WEIL

*After great pain, a formal feeling comes.*
EMILY DICKINSON

In the last chapter, I suggested that practice in being brave can alleviate some portion of pain. Of course, there is much more to it than that!

There are days when I don't want to admit that pain exists anywhere. I just don't feel up to it! There are other days when I can't do much about it—I simply hurt though I'd much rather not. As others have, no doubt, I have feared pain, hated it, fought it, fled it.

Our society has heightened our fear of pain. The media insist that not only is pain to be avoided, but that, if pain dares to appear, it is to be instantly medicated away. Further, the implication is that there is something psychologically abnormal about us if we accept pain. Comfort is what we believe in. It's almost an addiction.

Within limits, comfort-seeking is natural enough. But I don't think such a view of life is realistic. Worse, chronic comfort leaves us with minimal resources for using pain when it does come.

And it will come. Pain is an ordinary part of human experience. We may expect to be in pain at least part of the time. We will never like it, but we are fully human only if we experience it. There is no way we can always avoid pain. If we don't hurt today, we will hurt on another day.

Pain may come for a short visit or a long one. It seems to me that, since we *are* going to hurt, we may as well hurt for something worthwhile. We may as well use, not waste, the pain life brings.

My effort to understand and use pain began some thirty years ago in the dentist's chair. From that I moved to trying to understand and use emotional pain, since it seemed to dominate my feelings. I guess understanding helps me learn how to be responsible.

Reluctantly, I've learned that all pain has a purpose. It alerts us to something that is amiss. We feel pain when something is not right, whether bodily or emotionally or perhaps spiritually. However, we tend to regard the pain itself as our enemy and battle it directly. We often do not trouble to discover the pain's message, so we can do something about its cause.

When we race to the pill bottle or do other tricks to relieve pain, we may be only fighting, instead of using, our pain. Sometimes these temporary helps are useful; but sooner or later, it is better to find the cause of our pain and take action there. That's what pain is for. If there is an enemy, it is at the root of the pain; it is not the pain itself. So pain's first offer is to point us in the direction of the thing we need to see.

The second and often better opportunity that pain brings is ours only when the pain is going to be with us a while. Surely the more lasting the pain is, the less we like it; but it is still a fact that lasting pain gives us a stronger chance to use our unique power of choice. We ourselves can *decide* how lasting pain will serve us, if we let it.

Besides choices, God gave us another power that we rarely use and that is equally valuable: the power of attention. Usually our attention is "caught" by stimulation: the TV, another person, a beautiful view, an upsurge of emotion. Pain also is a stimulus that catches our attention. If we have banged an elbow, we notice that elbow. We are suddenly aware of its every nerve. Then we pay attention to what we do with that arm until the pain quits. The beginnings of emotional pain may not be as noticeable—or they may be quite dramatic—but emotional pain will also demand attention.

The trouble is that "caught" attention influences us in ways we may not suspect and might not even want. There's an old saying, "what gets your attention, gets *you*." Attention may lend power to the thing attended to, unless our own purpose is larger, a definite intention.

Attention can channel so much power that I have begun to be more careful about how I use it. It was at a time of deep emotional pain that I discovered how pain can call forth a quality of attention in me that can be both powerful and creative. It was hard to let that happen and it still is, but the effort is worth it.

When the pain of the situation in question seemed about to overwhelm me, I began to be quite careful about my whole self. I didn't think I could take much more; and so, very self-protectingly, I began to attend less to the pain and more to myself. Then I found a part of me that can *attend deliberately*. From that place within myself, I can observe what is going on. In that unfamiliar place, I felt—well, not quite peaceful, but rather neutral and somehow *able*, as if the pain simply couldn't touch me there. In that place of steady attention, there was a different sense of myself. I felt calmer and stronger there. It seems that this power of attending is nearer to my true self than any other part of me. Pain directed me toward it, and pain helped me stay with it until I discovered that place of quiet self-observation.

In reality, our true self, our deep self, is beyond our pain. "Beyond" does not mean that we do not feel the pain. It means that our *self* is in a different "place," where pain is felt, but does not dominate.

I recall that as my mother was dying, the nurses had to keep reinserting IV needles. Her skin seemed so fragile, so I asked Mom if that hurt. She said, "Not to any significant degree." I laughed because it was so like her: she did not identify her *self* with her pain. It was merely a sensation that she experienced and nothing more.

Stephen Levine, who has worked almost magically for decades with people in pain, has written that we can allow our pain to "float" in our awareness of our own being. Our own being is always larger and stronger than we may imagine. When we become quiet and attentive before our pain, when we gradually allow our resistance to dissolve, the pain is just another fact. It is not so significant as our being itself. Focusing on the deeper reality, we can allow the pain to be present and to give us its knowledge.

One way to do this, Levine says (and it works!) is consciously to focus on the area of pain and *soften* around it. Imagine the flesh softening. Let the inner gaze soften with compassion or mercy as we regard the pain within. Let the

whole body soften, quiet down, ease into a kindly attention toward itself. This softening in the face of pain is a
result of practice for most of us, not an immediate skill.
Even practicing opens splendid possibilities for peacefulness in pain and for the expansion of love.

As I write this, I have a painful mouth. I have new braces
on my teeth and they hurt all the time. So I practice being
soft with my pain, letting the gums "go soft" around it. I
can also use the mouth pain to remind me to attend to
something else—gratitude for the medical skills of my
orthodentist or even God's concern and love for me. Using
the opportunity presented by my pain, I can attend to these
other, more important things.

Each one of us will make the precise discoveries that we
need, if we practice relating to the pain instead of claiming
it as our own. We don't want to identify with the pain and
then resist it. We want to feel it and hear its messages.

One of the most fruitful discoveries for me has been a shift
in the quality of my inner attention. It doesn't happen regularly, but seems to appear when inner conditions are just
right. For short moments, I can see the quality of attention
itself. This may sound like trying to look at my own face without a mirror; but at special moments, something in me sees
my attention. I can briefly attend to that center of creative
power. Then joy may burst forth or peace blossom out or
clarity emerge or love arise. These are the deeper fruits of
attention and its promise of creativity in life. I would not want
to miss them. Only attention makes it possible for them to
appear, and a wonderful opportunity for that attention is
offered by pain. It's not the way I might prefer, but it works.

These moments of noticing our very attention can be re-
peated without pain, but that achievement is more difficult. Centered attention is the core of contemplative prayer

and leads directly to God's image deep within. The *practice* of attention is the basic skill of spiritual growth.

The practice of such attention is necessary for deep, quiet prayer—attention without words or images. Buddhists call it "bare attention" because, stripped of every usual object, it is just that—attention and nothing else. Attention to God (who cannot be adequately explained or pictured) seems bare. God can meet us without the hindrance of a racing mind.

A few years ago, I lost someone I dearly loved. The grief went its way through me, as grief must do in a healthy person. My every pore seemed saturated with its pain. It didn't go away for a long time. I cried and prayed, knowing that it would eventually get better—if I survived until then!

During that process, I became aware, ever so slowly, of something happening which I had not chosen, but have since been able to choose: I became not only more sensitive, but gentler. The pain, unresisted, was softening something inside me that needed to be softened. Beauty touched me more poignantly and easily. Other people's pain moved me to a new caring. I became more careful with words, with touching. I began almost to tiptoe through my days, gently but vibrantly alive to myself and everything near me.

The Old Testament prophets are full of this insight. We do not find it attractive. Still, if we don't get stuck at the painful part, we see that the prophets revealed something worth knowing about God and about us. It is this:

Usually, we are hard of heart. We are neither pliable to God nor gentle with ourselves. We do not follow God's ways easily, and we lie to ourselves about ourselves and about our following God. We all know how often we agree with God's Word but do not *do* it. The prophets say—in bold language—that God will send suffering to his people because of their hard hearts, *in a last-ditch effort to soften those hearts!*

God promises to replace stony hearts with natural hearts (Ezekiel 11:19-20). Ordinary life may not soften us easily, or we don't let it. But pain can. We know now that what God expressed through the prophets was not the desire for vengeance, but what we call today "tough love." We *need* gentle hearts to be fully human; and if we refuse them, God may let us suffer until they soften. We cannot understand this process with our reasoning alone. We must *let* pain do its work in us and seek to experience its benefits without rebellion. Then we will know, for it will happen.

It is rather like what happens when I have a headache. I walk carefully to avoid worsening it. Inner pain insists that I walk gingerly, more attentively. Since I have always been defensive and self-protective, it is wonderful that this sensitivity is led to express itself in caring and gentleness.

Attention is steadier when there is an inner gentleness, when I am softer, when I'm not spending energy in self-protection. Being softer means being more receptive, more open. It means being able to receive a "natural heart," a soft heart, full of love from the Lord.

From my first experience of gentleness, I wanted that gentleness to stay; so I tried to get acquainted with it. I let my pain guide me to a lasting awareness of my own capacity to be gentle with life. It was indeed good news! And I was able to hold on to enough of it to grow in tenderness. I am not always gentle now, but I am always more gentle than before. Sometimes I can allow gentleness to flow through me even without the help of pain. It's wonderful!

The mystic saints, such as Saint John of the Cross, have always praised suffering. For years that made no sense to me. Suffering seemed evil, and I could not see it any other way. I would have liked to think those saints were all masochists. But now I begin to understand, through my experience with pain, what the saints may have meant.

Pain urges me to attend. Pain heightens my sensitivity. It encourages me to soften not only with the pain, but with all of life. I become gentler with myself and with life and with God. I become more open, more careful and attentive. I cherish more. I receive more of God's goodness.

It is for this fruit of pain that I am most grateful. It would have been wonderful if I could have learned gentleness without pain. Nevertheless, just as the saints have said, pain (or suffering) was the big help. Why that seems necessary, I don't know. But I know it works. For now, that is enough.

If your pain is short-term, the fruit may not be quickly obvious. But these steps may be good practice anyway. Practice with short-term pain will likely be easier and that in itself will strengthen you. If your pain is going to last a while, please don't waste it. Decide to look deeply into the pain, for the source of the attention and gentleness your heart needs.

Here are the steps that have helped me.

- *Accept the pain as a normal fact.* It is there. It does hurt. Don't deny it. Even if you could convince yourself, denial is wasteful. Don't fight the pain. Don't blame yourself. Pain does not imply that something is amiss with your *self*. Resistance and blame take energy you need to attend to the pain and to soften around it—to do the work that pain asks you to do. Just admit clearly, "Yes, the pain really does hurt."
- *Watch the pain.* Notice it. See how the pain works in you. What does it do? Where does the pain lodge? You may also ask about its causes. If you can change them, you will want to. If you can't change the causes, then let the pain teach you about yourself. How does your body react to pain? How do you protect yourself? How are you affected by pain?

- *Talk to the pain.* Ask it to tell you about itself and its cause. Ask the pain what uses it might have prepared for you. Speak gently to the pain, with mercy in your heart. Then listen calmly to its messages. They will arise in your awareness when you are serene and sincere.
- *Notice what emotions the pain gives rise to.* Do you feel fear? Anger? Both? Perhaps helplessness? Irritability? Watch these emotions. For the moment, don't try to change them. They are a part of you—though only a part. Get to know them. If nothing else, you will be better prepared for the next time you hurt. Be patient, both with the pain and with the emotions you feel. *Let them be* in you.

  Above all, don't try too soon to "handle" the pain by pious notions like "giving it all to God." For some people, at some times, that surely can help. If it does, fine. But unless you are well-practiced at letting go, a time of intense discomfort is not the time to try to do it all at once. Especially leave this practice alone if your reason for attempting it is "I know I should give it all to God, but…"

  I often find it helpful to pray for insight and for strength not to waste the pain. Practicing being in the present moment *only* and softening around the pain helps a lot. I find it difficult to genuinely let go until my emotions have had their due. God will still be around, and there will be plenty of time to "give it all to God" when I can do it authentically and not just in words.
- *Soften your body and your mind around the pain.* Allow the pain space to be there. Be kind in your regard of it, as if it were another being. Allow the pain, and be merciful in your attitude. Let it "float" in your awareness.
- *Decide what you want this pain to do for you.* The pain may have clear ideas of its own; if you have watched carefully, you may already know what they are. It is wise to follow

pain's suggestions. If you discover none, you may come up with some ideas of your own. You may let the pain help you to act. Pain can be an effective motive. Or you may wish to let pain teach you about your power of attention. You just may decide to change yourself. Good! That's how growth happens.

- *Don't hurry any pain you feel, and don't be nasty to it.* Let the pain flow; let it complete its work in you. You will be "gentled" of necessity, because only in gentleness can you bear pain. If compassion for the world and its creatures results from your own pain—what a blessing! If you feel more vulnerable you are blessed again, because you will be able to receive more of beauty, more of love, more of God.

- *Let the pain direct your attention to prayer.* In the beginning, this prayer may be a simple but emphatic, "Help, God!" That's fine. As you practice being soft with the pain instead of resisting, however, you may find that you easily want to talk with the Lord about your experience. You may wish to ask God for help, for insight, for strength (not to resist, but to accept, remember!). As your attention becomes quieter and more steady, you may simply turn in God's direction and focus on our loving Lord instead of on the pain. The pain can help hold your attention on God. Then the possibility of a deeper experience of God is immediately open to you.

Attention guided by pain is purifying, like gold in fire. As you are more purified, you can receive more of God. Love has more room within. If life is for knowing and enjoying God, let's use whatever pain comes along to further our desire for God. Let us be willing to join our experience with Paul's words: "I consider that the sufferings of this present time are not worth comparing with the glory about to be revealed to us" (Romans 8:18).

## Suggestions for Prayer

Here is a suggested prayer format to get you started:

*Gentle God, I am hurting. And I don't like suffering. But pain is really there, so please help me not to waste it. I don't want to go through this for nothing. I want the experience to bear fruit within me. I want this pain to help me know you better and be closer to you. Help me to learn its lessons. Help me to soften and be gentle with myself in this experience. Help me not to resist with rigidity. Help me to choose the best way to respond to hurt, so that my desire for you may come closer to fulfillment.*

Someday you may be able to thank God for the pain you now feel. You may be able to do it now. If so, do thank God. But don't lie. When the time comes that you can thank God truly and freely—and only then—don't miss the chance!

## Scripture Suggestions

*Psalm 40:4*
Happy are those who make the LORD their trust, who do not turn to the proud, to those who go astray after false gods.

*Proverbs 17:3*
The crucible is for silver, and the furnace is for gold,
   but the LORD tests the heart.

*Wisdom 3:1-3*
But the souls of the righteous are in the hand of God,
and no torment will ever touch them.
In the eyes of the foolish they seemed to have died,

and their departure was thought to be a disaster,
and their going from us to be their destruction;
but they are in peace.

Here are some additional Scriptures for further reflection.

*Psalm 77:1-15*    *Matthew 12:18-21*    *Hebrews 5:8-9*
*Psalm 86:1-13*    *Romans 8:16-18*      *1 Peter 2:19-23*

## For Reflection

The following exercises may be useful to you as an opportunity for self reflection:

- Place your hands on the area of pain (yes, emotional pain often focuses on a specific physical area). Project gentleness, love, tenderness, and acceptance through your hands onto your pain. (Note: Be cautious, however. It is lovely to wish healing for ourselves, when that wish is not a form of resistance to the pain that is there. In this exercise, it may be better just to send mercy and tenderness to the area of pain than to try to get the pain to change.)
- Ask questions of the pain, and answer them aloud. Go gently and listen with an open heart. Give no advice to yourself, but just respond and then go on to next question.
- Imagine that you are taking the pain in your cupped hands. Hold it with utter gentleness. Speak to it quietly, all together. Then lift your hands, still cupped, upward, and say, "Lord, this is my pain. I'm willing to keep the pain or lose it, according to your purposes for me. Let me not waste it."

$\mathcal{C}$HAPTER $\mathcal{T}$HREE

# DON'T LET FEAR
# RUN YOUR LIFE

*You gain strength, courage, and confidence
by every experience in which you really stop
to look fear in the face.*
ELEANOR ROOSEVELT

*Fear keeps us chattering—fear that wells up
from the past, fear of blurting out what we really fear,
fear of future repercussions.
It is our very fear of the future that distorts
the now that could lead to a different future
if we dared to be whole to the present.*
MARION WOODMAN

*Feel the fear, then let it go. Jump in
and do it—whatever it is. If our instincts
and path have led us there, it's where we need to be.*
MELODIE BEATTIE

The tree was some seventy feet tall, or so they said afterward. Twenty of us were grouped near its base, wearing hard hats and harnesses. The tree's branches had been stripped and replaced by heavy spikes, carefully placed at awkward distances apart. At about twelve feet from the top of the tree hung a large metal ring, slung on a rope from other trees. The challenge presented to us was to climb to the top of the tree and then leap for the ring. Our leader said there was no danger since a belaying rope would be attached to our harnesses, and the belayer would stop our probable fall in midair.

Looking up—far up—at that ring, I knew the leader told the truth. If he hadn't, this whole workshop could not have existed. Everything he said made complete sense—to my head. My insides, however, did *not* get the message.

I was afraid. Fear spread rapidly from my midsection to my arms and legs. Before it could paralyze me, I stepped forward and said (as required), "My name is Marilyn and I choose to do this event. And I'm very scared!"

The stakes in the tree were far apart for my short legs. I was trembling. I might have quit ten feet up had the group not been yelling nonstop encouragement. One stake at a time, I climbed the slender, increasingly wavering tree. It seemed to take forever, yet I arrived on the top stake too soon. The ring looked a football field away, out there in the (gulp!) air. Gazing at it, trying not to look down, I went rigid with terror. But the group kept cheering for me. I hesitated a long time up there.

Suddenly, I felt angry at myself for being so afraid. I chose. Slowly, carefully, I crouched down against the tree, my hands encircling it behind me. Then with a glance at the belayer so far below, I hurled myself forward as hard as I could. I missed the ring. For an eye-closed moment, I dropped. Then the belaying rope caught and I floated to the ground, euphoric. As my toes touched, the group buried me in warm hugs. Exhilaration rushed through me and I felt I could have flown back up to that ring.

The experiment took only a few minutes, but I learned a lesson for life. And I learned it *in my body*, where I was less likely to forget it than learning purely in my mind. Later, reflecting on the experience, I noticed several wonderful things.

First, I found a new, sure confidence that *fear* would never again make a decision for me. I have always been afraid. Since I was a child, fear has hindered me nearly every day. Fear may never leave me entirely. But since that day on the tree, I know that even though fear may come, it will never again make any choices for me. I will decide for myself, and never because I'm scared. I have chosen against fear's domination—permanently.

Second, I noticed that *when I moved, the fear disappeared.* I acted and I was freed of fear. That's worth knowing. The ability to act (to leap, in my case), was triggered by the group support and by my own disgust with myself for being so unreasonably terrified. For other people the trigger may be different. One of my companions in this experience was a small woman who was intensely afraid of heights. Her decision to leap was triggered by humor. When she was paralyzed at the top, someone called out, "Hey! Make like Tarzan and go!" The tiny woman laughed, gave a mighty yell, and leaped. Her fear, too, vanished. Action takes fear's energy and directs it to better uses.

Third, I was keenly aware of *deciding to trust* the belayer and the inventor of this wild apparatus. I accepted what my common sense told me instead of what my fear told me. I trusted that the belayer would catch me before bones got smashed.

Today these three points, lodged forever in my body, seem to form a whole. That whole helps me live confidently in spite of being afraid. Because I learned that I can choose, and because I accepted responsibility for creating the quality of my experience, I began to examine my own fearfulness. What did it contribute to the quality of my life? Well, fear didn't seem to contribute much that I wanted to keep. It did keep me out of the way of trucks and such. It also held me back from some experiences that could enrich my life. So, I didn't want fear to have so much power in my life anymore.

For that, a deeper understanding of fear was necessary. Dr. Gerald Jampolsky, a psychiatrist who works with children with catastrophic diseases and their families, was a big help. He says there are really only two basic emotional realities: fear and love. Love is outward-oriented, and it is basic to our nature. Fear turns us in on ourselves. It is an ego-centered reaction. Fear shuts our hearts, distorts our perceptions of what's really happening. So, Jampolsky points out, when we choose not to be controlled by fear, we open our hearts. We clear our perceptions. Inside ourselves is now a space for love to appear. It is a basic choice and a powerful one, a choice to be true to our own deepest selves.

That sounded good. The next discovery was that fear stimulates a lot of energy. We have physical and mental energies, and then a pool of energy that seems for a moment to have no specific quality at all. It is just there. If fear captures that neutral energy, it drives us in a turned-in-on-ourselves direction or in a runaway direction. In other words, when frightened, we find the energy either to protect ourselves or to flee, maybe bodily, maybe in feelings and words. When the fright takes over the energy it has stimulated, fear determines what our actions will be.

But that take-over by fear need not happen. The power of responsible choice is greater than the power of fear. I can *always* choose between love and fear. As soon as I feel afraid, I must claim that available energy and decide what purpose I want it to serve. Choice is not emotion. It is not destroyed by emotion. I can do what I choose with the energy of fear. I can use it for action—I *can* leap freely for the ring.

My choice will be strengthened by a turn toward trust. By turning away from fear, I turn toward love and toward trust, which is love's first cousin. Trust usually needs a focus. For leaping from seventy-foot trees, I trust a skillful belayer. For remaining in a roomful of strangers, I trust my ability to respond to whatever is said to me. For learning a new skill, I trust a teacher who knows. For trying to practice Jesus' advice about life, I trust God to help.

A caution is necessary here: the decision to trust should not be blind. To trust does not mean assuming that nothing hurtful can happen. To trust is to choose to believe that whatever happens, I can handle it "with a little help from my friends" and a lot of help from God. Knowing the secret of not wasting pain helps me trust even more easily, because I know there is beauty to be created from almost any risk undertaken in trust.

When a decision is made to trust and then to act, a special transformation occurs. Fear quickly gives way to a high sense of adventure. The results are always satisfying and sometimes spectacular. I remember Don, who as a young man was terrified by blood, his own and other people's. Twice he fainted when someone nearby was injured. He could have been helpful if he hadn't been so scared. He was embarrassed and distressed at his limitation. He didn't like the choice that fear was making for him. So he set about "adventuring" with his fear, though he confesses it wasn't much fun at first. He began by reading about blood—what it's made of and how it works in the body, its symbolic meaning in literature and religion. He gradually began to sense a new feeling, a reverence for blood. He became fascinated.

But he had yet to confront blood directly. He made a plan. He would act. He would prick his own finger and observe the blood. At the very thought, his fear roared at him. "I will do it anyway," he insisted. Then he lay on the bed so he wouldn't hurt himself if he fainted! By affirming "I know that looking at blood can't hurt me," he trusted what he already knew, though fear spread through his whole body.

He decided to channel the fear-energy into determination. So, in spite of a few light-headed moments, he remained conscious and observed his own droplet of blood. He recalled all he'd read about it. Suddenly the drop seemed a thing of wonder. When he finally wiped it away, he knew his fear might return, but never so overwhelmingly. He was free to choose; he had taken over his fear's energy and made it serve his own purposes.

For Don, the surprising adventure began when he found himself still interested in the thing he once feared. Today he is a doctor, specializing in the circulatory system. Fear, faced and mastered, helped him discover his profession.

Don discovered the secret of choice beyond fear and it rewarded him. No, I have not made a profession of leaping from tall trees. But Don and I, in our separate ways, found that fear is, in fact, an opportunity to capture our own energy and direct it where we truly want it to be effective. Fear is a chance to act trustfully by choice and thus to create more beauty in our lives.

Fear closes us off from love, and so from God. If our hearts long for God and we cling to our fears—giving them our power of choice—we cannot live close to God's heart. If we choose to free ourselves from fear's domination, we will find God where he always waits: right in our own hearts.

Fear seems to speed up our thinking. So the steps that follow are too slow for any initial crisis. But you can practice on any chronic fear you have—fear of new people, fear of making a mistake, or any fear you may be aware of.

- *First, when you feel fear, name it.* Say, "I am afraid of..." Make it definite. Many times you will feel a little silly right away, because you know the thing that scares you isn't really threatening. If there is a deeper fear, look for it and name it. For example, "I'm afraid of speaking to a group because I'm afraid they won't like me."
- *Notice the direction the fear will take if it decides for you.* If you are afraid of new people, for instance, you may never get to know anyone you don't already know; and you see that this will make your future life poorer. Or, you are afraid of making mistakes, so you will never try anything new. Thus you won't grow and won't be able to help anyone else much either. When you see the direction your fear tends to take you, you may immediately know you don't want it to run your life any more.
- *When you feel afraid, take a moment to notice the energy in your body.* You are fired up to do something! In fact, you may hardly be able to sit still.
- *Claim that energy for your own and choose to direct it by action where you truly want it to go.* Marcie, a young mother of three, was afraid to move to a new town because she didn't know anyone there and she had never moved before. But she did want the professional opportunity that was available there. So she channeled her fear-energy into creating a lovely new home and getting started in her new work. By the time her fear-energy was spent, she

was more effective in the new place than she had imagined possible. Her homesickness was almost gone too. The energy stimulated by her fears had powered a new and beautiful life. You can do the same, whether your change is big or small.

- *Find someone or something to trust in.* Or trust in what is already known. In leaping from the tree, I trusted in the belayer and the ongoing program. A hiker found the courage to walk a log across a raging river, because he trusted in the strength of a friend's hand. It may be your own experience that you trust, or a friend, a family member, or God. Before you act, pause a few moments to remember in whom or in what you trust. Give thanks for that.

- *Now spend no more time thinking. Choose! Act!* Go into action. Your discoveries from here on are your own. They'll be exciting and life-renewing. Count on it. You will be freer because fear need never control your choices again. And God will be closer in your experience than ever before.

## Suggestions for Prayer

An excellent form of prayer at any time, and especially when choosing around our own fears, is prayer that is quiet and relaxing. For quiet prayer, we relax the body deeply, keeping the spine straight. We relax the thoughts, guiding them gently toward peaceful scenes or lovely memories. Then we allow ourselves caringly to become aware of the presence of God or the love of Jesus or the tenderness of Mary. We rest in this presence, enjoying the relaxation and feeling the goodness, the safety of this quiet. Then, ever so softly, we make the steps listed above in a serene conversation with God. We tell God each one, ask for blessings on each step and affirm our trust in the Lord. When we are finished, we remain still a little while, to allow time for spontaneous gratitude. Then, slowly, we return—ready to act on our peace-filled prayer.

## Scripture Suggestions

*Deuteronomy 31:6*
"Be strong and bold; have no fear or dread of them, because it is the LORD your God who goes with you."

*1 Chronicles 28:20*
"David said further to his son Solomon, 'Be strong and of good courage, and act. Do not be afraid or dismayed; for the LORD God, my God, is with you. He will not fail you or forsake you, until all the work for the service of the house of the LORD is finished.'"

*Psalm 34:7-8*
The angel of the LORD encamps
   around those who fear him, and delivers them.
O taste and see that the LORD is good;
   happy are those who take refuge in him.
O fear the LORD, you his holy ones,
   for those who fear him have no want.

*Psalm 56:4-5*
In God, whose word I praise,
   in God I trust; I am not afraid;
   what can flesh do to me?
All day long they seek to injure my cause;
   all their thoughts are against me for evil.

*Proverbs 3:5-6*
Trust in the Lord with all your heart,
    and do not rely on your own insight.
In all your ways acknowledge him,
    and he will make straight your paths.

*Matthew 10:26-28*
"So have no fear of them; for nothing is covered up that
will not be uncovered, and nothing secret that will not become known. What I say to you in the dark, tell in the light;
and what you hear whispered, proclaim from the housetops.
Do not fear those who kill the body but cannot kill the soul;
rather fear him who can destroy both soul and body in hell."

*1 John 4:18*
There is no fear in love, but perfect love casts out fear; for
fear has to do with punishment, and whoever fears has not
reached perfection in love.

Here are some additional Scriptures for further reflection.

| *Psalm 23* | *Psalm 125:1-2* | *Hebrews 13:5-8* |
| *Psalm 57* | *Isaiah 40:28-31* | *2 Timothy 1:7* |

## For Reflection

Find a place of solitude and think about these topics:

- my most chronic fear
- my most powerful fear
- a time when I chose to let my fear be there, and acted on
  a deeper choice

# CHANNEL ANGER CREATIVELY

*My mother used to say,*
*"He who angers you, conquers you!"*
SISTER ELIZABETH KENNY

*People who fly into a rage*
*always make a bad landing.*
WILL ROGERS

Today the sun is shining and everything is peaceful. Anger seems very far away. But only last week I boiled over about something. Though it doesn't happen often anymore, I can never know for sure when anger will erupt.

I am firmly convinced that anger is not necessary to our lives. It is an avoidable, egotistical emotion of which Jesus himself did not approve (see Matthew 5:21-23).

"Ooops! Wait a minute!" you may wish to object. "What about the cleansing of the Temple?" Here the difficulty is in ourselves: it is difficult to imagine such strong action taken in complete determination, but free of anger. The New Testament calls it "zeal."

Recently when a friend insisted that Jesus, too, got angry, I asked him why he wanted to think of Jesus as angry. Honest as always, this man paused and then said, "Self-justification! Proves nothing, huh?" Precisely.

Because we do not understand our own anger and seldom know how it arises or what better uses we might find for it, we think it is human and therefore that everybody gets mad. Everyone *can* be angry; *not* everyone does get angry.

Ponder for a few moments the basic causes of anger. There are really only three fundamental reasons for getting angry. Think about the triggers for your own anger for a minute, then see how they fit into these three reasons:

1. Fear. When we are afraid, we may get angry to cover it or get angry at the thing/person that frightened us.
2. Pain. We get angry when something hurts us.
3. Frustration over not getting our own way. When we are  thwarted or stopped in our plans, we are likely to strike out in anger, at least inside ourselves.

Once we see what underlies our anger, we can again ask about Jesus. Do we also think he got angry because of fear? We see in the Passion story that he was not at all angry over pain. What about Jesus not getting his own way—would that make him mad?

Experience has taught me that anger is subject to training and to choice. I can decide to be angry or not in a given circumstance *if* I am attentive enough to myself. That is the hard part. The moment when I choose to be angry or not is only a flash, and if I miss it, anger takes control. Then it feels as if I "can't help" getting mad. That little phrase really means that I chose anger (by default probably) so fast that I didn't notice choosing.

Since I decide not to be angry only when I'm very attentive, realistically I will continue to feel angry sometimes. So will most of us, right? That probability simply tells us that we're not as mature as Jesus Christ was. That shouldn't surprise us! Nor should we condemn ourselves for it. We can use the recognition of our immaturity as a spur to growth.

So, let's reflect on our anger as it actually occurs. When we get angry, what happens next? Do we admit our angry feelings *and* express them as some popular psychology tells us to?

Denial of feelings is dangerous to emotional health. *Pious* denial endangers spiritual life as well. If anger is roiling and I say, "I'm not angry," that is simply a lie, to self and to God. My anger then will turn against my body and may make me sick.

We *need* to admit to ourselves and to God the way things really are inside us. God is Truth as well as Love. We need to be truthful too. Besides, God already knows how things really are, and is ready to help us do something constructive with our anger-energies.

Recent psychological studies show that many times the *expression* of anger intensifies it. By acting "mad," we get "madder!" If these studies are right, then it may not always be helpful to yell ugly words or pound pillows. We can find out for ourselves by watching the effects of our own anger when we express it or when we don't. Try it out and see!

Like fear, anger stimulates a large amount of energy that is then available. Think how spent you felt after your last blowup. For what did all that energy go?

Anger need not make our decisions. We are not victims of our own emotions if we do not wish to be. We need to learn how to channel anger-energies toward what we really want. This is completely possible—and it's possible every time. It may not be easy anytime.

Though anger is a result of and expresses our self-centeredness, it may bring with it other feelings that at first seem like benefits. An explosion of anger may make us feel strong. It may give us safe feelings, as if we were protected by emotion. It may give us a feeling of control. These feelings, however, are temporary. They seldom create the effect we want. Some people do keep anger because they want those other feelings. Still, the decision to do so is based on an illusion.

Anger, when unchecked by responsible choice, heightens our self-centeredness. There are not-yet-mature people for whom expression of anger may be a necessary step toward independence. If you are one of these, you must respect where you stand and give yourself a chance to grow. For many adults, an ego that keeps expanding, dominating, insisting on more and more choices and actions, is a barrier to spiritual growth. Self-centeredness is at the core of our sinfulness. The things which separate us from God simultaneously keep us limited to our own selfish ways of thinking and acting. If we make an effort to reduce our self-centeredness, we create a new and lovely openness within ourselves. It is filled with potential for beauty.

When we choose not to let anger control our actions by preempting our decisions, we resist the self-centered part of ourselves. That is the moment God waits for. The response to that inner openness is certain: God will fill that openness and give us as much as we can receive and need. It may be a warm feeling toward someone who has angered us or a new understanding of a destructive pattern left over from our childhood. God may give us an awareness of our own creativity, deepen our love, or draw us to quiet prayer. Whatever the gift, God's response to our decision not to be angry is ours to keep.

So the "trick" we can learn is to notice our anger and to channel its energies into our true purposes, that is, into creating the quality of life we want when we are not full of angry emotions.

For example, I want warm, open relationships with other people. When I get angry, I'm likely to be highly defensive. Defensiveness doesn't help toward open friendships! Others get aggressive or mean when they are angry. I can decide not to explode, but to turn the energy to sorting out what happened between me and my friends. That may mean saying nothing for a while, then directly opening the subject and kindly inviting their view of what happened. It's not easy. The ego will sting. My body sometimes trembles with the effort! But anger need not control me, because I do not want it to. The result is what I really want: friendly, mutual understanding.

Often, anger is triggered by some specific thing. That anger fades as quickly as the matter is let go. There is also chronic anger. It requires more attention. Chronic anger may be left over from childhood hurts or come from needs chronically unmet. It may have other causes. Sometimes it helps to find the cause of chronic anger, and for this, professional help may be useful. Some people are able to discover by themselves how their anger works at present, and these insights are sufficient enough to proceed.

Though my outbursts of anger made me want to understand it and to discover Jesus' view of it, it was my chronic anger that had the most to offer me. When I began to choose to be responsible, I noticed that many of my habits and responses did not work well for me. By that I mean that they didn't contribute to the quality of life I wanted. I wanted more inner freedom, more creativity, more growth, deeper relationships, more capacity for loving. Observing my chronic anger, I saw that it scattered its tremendous energy in fruitless, tense criticism of things I couldn't change. So I began to quit saying those things and instead decided to change my own attitudes, habits, and actions.

Determination fueled by anger can be a strong force. A British seminary professor told a story of his student days in England during World War II. The bombing of Britain had begun. One day while he was in the library studying Hebrew, the air raid alarm sounded; he was supposed to join the others racing for shelter. But this time he got mad. He sat there pounding his desk, saying, "Damn it! When this is over *someone* has got to know Hebrew!" And he stayed, furiously memorizing Hebrew verbs while the planes roared over! Soon his Hebrew was excellent.

If that student could use his "mad" energies for learning Hebrew during a bombing, so can we use ours for whatever purposes we choose. If our anger tends to turn outward, we may decide to change something around us: rearrange the house, initiate changes in our community, seek a different job, get training in an area of interest. When our anger turns in on ourselves, we can use it to change a habit, to stop nagging the kids, to listen to others more carefully, or to put our body daily in a quiet place to pray. The purpose into which any individual decides to channel anger-energy is entirely his or her own choice. The important thing is that the redirected anger-energy contributes to the quality of life and the strength of the relationship being created. And if something still doesn't work, another choice is always available.

There's a strange law in life: whenever we begin to learn something new, with openness, life gives us big opportunities to practice it. It happened to me when I began learning to channel anger creatively. I was studying for a doctorate and had been working hard for several months on a presentation that would determine the direction and success of my studies. The day before the presentation was due, I took it to the department head for his final review. I'd been checking regularly with him for three months. He looked calmly at me and said, "You know this won't fly, don't you?" I was stunned. In my mind I saw months of work wasted.

"Why not?" I asked, beginning to churn inside. He explained in three short sentences. Instantly I could see that he was right.

"Why didn't you point this out before?" I demanded, hardly believing he could be so mean as to leave this comment until the last minute. "I kept hoping you'd see it yourself," he said, smiling.

I can't describe the turmoil and fury that immediately arose. I was so angry I literally did not know what to do. Then, because I was afraid to antagonize this man, I left. By the time I reached my apartment, I was fuming, thrashing inside and wanting to thrash somebody else too. How could I possibly fix this presentation by the next day?

Then I *noticed* how roaring mad I was. I stood still. I reminded myself of my insights into channeling anger responsibly. Yes, I'd been dealt a bad card, but I could still decide how to play it. With great effort, I recalled the quality of creativity I wanted in this presentation. I didn't think it possible to do it overnight. I also realized that I couldn't do anything the least bit creative in my infuriated state.

My psychologist-brother had once said, "Always be gentle with yourself in a crisis." So I decided first to be nice to me.

I took myself to a favorite restaurant where I could watch the ocean and order everything my fancy suggested. I stared at the rippling water, trying to think of its beauty, of the food—anything but the problem. With determined attention, I enjoyed that meal. And I only allowed myself thirty seconds to question the money I was spending.

It seems impossible to stay mad when everything is peaceful and comfortable, even the stomach! So, gradually, I became calmer. And as I watched the rhythmic waves, an unexpected idea floated into my mind: the presentation *could* be changed; I could see how to do it; I knew whom to call for help with it. My anger now resurfaced as excitement about the new possibility. I rushed home to try it out.

To shorten the tale, the presentation was corrected in time and passed easily. More interesting still, the altered section became the most fascinating part of all my studies. That dinner money was extremely well-spent. My anger-energies, turned in a better direction, proved very creative.

Looking back over my life, I believe that my anger has changed. It is much less frequent and much milder. I believe there are four reasons for this: (1) I have chosen to be responsible and have quit looking for a fairy tale "fix" for my life; (2) I have tried hard to see and understand my own chronic anger; (3) As I chose to channel anger-energy into the qualities of living and relating that I really wanted, the habit of angry reaction has been weakened; (4) I have seen clearly that anger kept me from God. That is my strongest motivation to find the keys to an anger-free life. So I feel good about the energy that sometimes surges, threatening to become anger. It is useful. Sometimes anger still catches me inattentive and unaware, and sometimes I still yield my power of decision to this anger. But there has been profound growth, and I rejoice over that.

Here are a few steps that may be instrumental in channeling anger-energies.

- *Make a basic decision about anger.* You and you alone are able to choose about your emotions. Do you want your angry outbursts? Do they bring to your life what you want? If not, then you can decide to do different things with your anger-energies.
- *The next time you feel angry, try at that moment not to say or do anything.* (The person you're fighting with may be puzzled, but that's okay.) Notice the flow of energy in your body. How does it feel? Where is the energy located? You may wish to do this experiment several times, to get acquainted with your own emotion and its energy, as well as how it works. You might lose an argument or two, but so what? That helps reduce your egocentrism!
- *Look for the feelings that come with anger and seem to reward you.* That secondary payoff is delivered directly to your self-centeredness. Ask yourself if these rewards are real and if you want to keep them. Ask if more self-centered is what you want. Remember, the choice is entirely yours.
- *Choose an area of your life in which you'd like to grow and make creative changes.* Make a clear mental picture of what you have now, and of what you want. For the first experiment, choose something fairly simple, something that will give you quick and obvious results. It's often better to begin in areas where success is not difficult—the results encourage us while *they teach us.*
- *When you have chosen, begin to turn your anger-energies in that direction.* You might even try saying to the person you're mad at, "I feel angry right now, but I need these energies for something more important, so I won't discuss

this until later." You may wish to assure the person that you do not think she or he is unimportant, but only that your anger-energy is needed elsewhere. All kinds of wonders might happen if you tried something as honest as this!

- *Enjoy!* This is an exciting project. It will bring you rich and lasting rewards in personal integrity, personal strength, relationships with others, and in your prayer relationship with God. You will discover that this energy is truly yours to be sent with power in the direction you choose. You are no longer a victim of your own angry emotions. You are coming to freedom responsibly.

## *Suggestions for Prayer*

Every step mentioned previously, and the others you may discover, should be taken in prayer. This prayer is not exactly asking God to do something for you. God will not make your decisions, for example. But you do ask for blessings, for God's assistance in your process, and for insight. When this kind of work is done—and it is work—we need insight, we need honesty. We need the ability to step back and see ourselves, looking for information at first and putting evaluation on hold. We need to see how we are inside.

God will help us to do this. God is always on our side, offering compassion and promoting our growth. God supports our efforts. When we pray about our anger, we ask not that something be done for us, but that we be given the gift of insight, so that we can make wise and responsible choices.

The quieter we can be before God, the better. When we pray about anger-energies, we pray restfully, perhaps with pencil and paper nearby. Insights may need to be caught before they vanish. We thank God, too, especially for making us so that we need not be victimized by our angers, that we are able to live peaceful, anger-free lives, and that these energies are available for beautiful uses. We thank God for standing by us, for caring about us.

I find that it helps to take my anger to a trusted advisor. Not every counselor will respond as might be wished, because many do not view anger as an evil and a detriment. But acknowledging our anger is really for healing. Anger wounds. It wounds us more than we imagine. So the act of admitting anger opens us up to healing. We can distance ourselves a little from the anger too. Next time, it is easier to notice anger quickly and to channel it.

## Scripture Suggestions

*Psalm 39:1*
I said, "I will guard my ways
   that I may not sin with my tongue;
I will keep a muzzle on my mouth
   as long as the wicked are in my presence."

*Proverbs 11:12*
Whoever belittles another lacks sense,
   but an intelligent person remains silent.

*Proverbs 15:1,17-18*
A soft answer turns away wrath,
   but a harsh word stirs up anger....
Better is a dinner of vegetables where love is
   than a fatted ox and hatred with it.
Those who are hot-tempered stir up strife,
   but those who are slow to anger calm contention.

*Proverbs 17:14*
The beginning of strife is like letting out water;
   so stop before the quarrel breaks out.

*Matthew 5:22*
"But I say to you that if you are angry with a brother or sister, you will be liable to judgment; and if you insult a brother or sister, you will be liable to the council; and if you say, 'You fool,' you will be liable to the hell of fire."

Here are other Scripture references for reflection.

| | | |
|---|---|---|
| *Psalm 37:1-11* | *Proverbs 19:3* | *Proverbs 22:24-25* |
| *Psalm 98:1-9* | *Proverbs 21:14* | *Ephesians 4:26-27,31-32* |
| | *Proverbs 29:11* | *Colossians 3:8-10* |

## For Reflection

A self-analysis of the three basic reasons for anger—as outlined in this chapter—may be fruitful. If the question of "righteous anger or justifiable anger" arises, consider Jesus on the cross: would anger have been justified? What did Jesus choose instead?
   Consider the following questions:

- What triggers my anger?
- What might I personally do differently?
- Do I like anger? Why? (It is important to see this, because we can change only what we can see in ourselves.)

## CHAPTER FIVE

# LET OTHERS
# LIKE YOU

*You grow up the day you have
the first real laugh—at yourself.*
ETHEL BARRYMORE

*It is better that joy should be spread
over all the day in the form of strength
than it should be concentrated into ecstasies....*
RALPH WALDO EMERSON

The feeling is as vivid today as it was when I was five years old. Our family had moved, and my parents were unpacking boxes—some so big I could hardly see into them. Daddy got a bit frantic looking for the pliers he couldn't remember packing. I dug around and found them. His excited comment was, "You're worth five dollars!"

I was thrilled. I felt warmed all over. Five dollars sounded like five million; but best of all, someone important found me worthwhile.

Contrast that expansive, joyous feeling with the emotion of a woman who sat across from me nearly forty years later. She was crying. The emptiness inside her could be felt. Although she had plenty of money, she was sloppy—hair barely combed, clothes that didn't fit, overweight and uncared for. She had come to me about a problem, but it was easy to see that her "problem" was not the deepest source of her suffering. Her emptiness was rooted in a painful feeling of worthlessness, an assumption that she was not worthy to walk on the earth or to feel life in her veins, to express herself or to receive love.

She is far from alone. There are many, many people of all ages and types who, deep in their hearts, feel utterly unworthy of anything good. Our society acknowledges that feeling in many ways: support groups spring up; people seek individual therapy; we bolster ourselves with piles of possessions; we seek status and reassurance in every direction. The feeling of worthlessness haunts us.

Oddly, the people who feel the most worthless are often religious people, Christians. Surely Christianity was not meant to crush us like that! Christianity is *good* news.

Like many Christians, I have struggled with the gut-feeling that Christianity is something that I *must* live up to and that I must do perfectly right now, or better yet, that I should have been perfect yesterday. I assume that complete achievement is what God expects. But I am aware that I do not live up to the teachings of the New Testament or of my Church. I have not attained that achievement. Christian practice is usually a struggle; and though sometimes a happy one, it is not always successful. Yet this picture of perfection hangs before me. It doesn't feel like good news. It feels like an impossible demand that turns into a reproach because I don't meet it totally. And when I look at that, I feel unworthy.

I used to feed my feelings of unworthiness. Here's one of my "favorite oldie" habits—and not only mine: I would take one virtue from one great saint and another from someone else (contemplation from Saint John of the Cross, poverty from Saint Francis of Assisi, simplicity from the Little Flower, and so on, and so on) and mix them all together into one ideal human being. Then I'd compare myself to this imaginary character. No wonder I always came up short!

Then I would tear myself down for my obvious shortcomings, telling myself in a hundred ways how awful I was. I also shut out much of the love and warmth offered to me by other people, thinking that if they liked *me* they must be stupid. I must have mystified many potential friends!

Carl Rogers helped me here, simply by admitting to the same habit of not letting other people's appreciation into his insides. He said that he learned only gradually to "soak up" his dearness to others and their warm responses to him. He agreed with what I slowly uncovered: It is energizing to let others love me. It feels wonderful! The value they find in me can become value that I enjoy and believe in too.

Feeling worthless may be a normal response to our culture and our high ideals. But unworthiness is not life-giving; it does not make us healthy. Worthlessness as a habitual response is not necessary. It is another attitude we can choose to change.

I had to make that choice and then practice letting other people love me, letting them give to me, letting them appreciate me—and allowing all those luscious feelings to penetrate my heart. Other people offer a lot. I had missed so much by holding them at arm's length because of my own feelings of worthlessness. When, like Carl Rogers, I chose to let others delight in me, and to delight in their delight with me, I found a bonus. Now I could laugh at my own peculiarities and odd habits.

I can smile more easily now about the not-so-perfect parts of my personality. I can smile, too, about the lovely and good parts. I can finally acknowledge that I have considerable ability, that I am not insignificant. I can enjoy my talents and foster my own interests. They are the key to my particular contribution to life. And when I contribute, my feeling of worthiness rises.

Feeling worthless can be a kind of reverse ego-trip. When I feel rotten about myself, it may be easy to think I'm being "self-less." But the fact is that such feelings merely center me more on myself and usually add self-pity to my feelings. There is just nothing good about self-pity and nothing good about hating myself. These attitudes bring out nothing creative or loving in me. In fact, just the reverse. They prevent me from loving, they stifle creativity. Clinging to feeling rotten about myself or clinging to self-pity is like slamming a huge steel door, locking it down tight and throwing away the key. I can't get out and others can't get in. I need to choose to let go of feeling worthless and let go of self-pity.

As I practiced letting go of such feelings and letting others love me, I did begin to feel more worthy of life. But I also discovered a basic confusion in the way I thought and felt. It had to do with my feelings of worthlessness and my stature before God. I thought they were the same, but they are definitely not. Here is how I finally unscrambled them:

In Genesis 2:7, God blows the breath of life into his new creature, the human being. If God withdrew his breath from me even now, I would not exist. I would vanish. The simplest and most automatic human act, breathing, is completely dependent on God's presence to me and God's constant sustaining activity in me, whether or not I am aware of it. My existence is therefore not mine.

At that absolutely basic level, "I" am nothing. God is

everything. God is the Creator and I'm a completely dependent creature. Of myself I am nothing.

This insight has the quality of newness. It doesn't make me feel rotten. This understanding is a clear, unmuddied perception of something real. It has solidity, as if I could stand on it firmly balanced for life. This awareness is not an evaluation of myself. It is the *fact* of God's complete superiority. In this sense, my own nothingness in the face of God's greatness, deeper than thoughts or words, has become a touchstone for me. I return to it to get myself and my activities into perspective.

Of myself, then, I am lost unless God notices me. The good news of Christianity is that God notices me. God notices me so singularly and loves me so much that his Son, Jesus, came to live as I must live and to communicate the Father's compassion to me, to assure me of help, and to become that help for me. The good news of Christianity can be fully recognized when I have become aware of my own nothingness before God's all-powerfulness. Then everything in my life becomes not demand, but gift. That's a totally different perspective!

To God I am worth something—though why may always be a mystery locked in the Knower's heart. God made me and loves all creatures because of who the Creator is, not because of my qualities (bad or good). Look at this world! Look at my heart! Has this *earned* the Divine Compassion? Hardly. But God *is* compassion itself. So, although I am nothing of myself, God loves me into worthiness. Whether noticed or not, that love is the *only* foundation under my life.

There is another angle to this. We can acknowledge our fundamental nothingness without God. We can admit to ourselves that in fact we are, *all* of us, unworthy of the great compassion of the Lord. Then, right in the midst of this feeling, we can turn our hearts to God with this prayer: "Lord, I know I'm not worthy of you. Without your help, I will never be worthy. But even in my unworthiness, I long to experience your love. I long to know you. I so want everything you have to give me." This prayer is always answered, usually not suddenly, but little by little.

God loves me and all others together in the same way, accounting every one of us worthy to be on earth, to live. God put us here! God knows we are deeply good. Therefore, I am as worthy as all others to receive love and to grow toward God. No one else is left out of this divine love, either.

Genesis 1:26-27 tells us that we are created in God's own image. Something in us is like God. That something is at the center of our being. It hasn't anything to do with the countries we live in, the professions we choose, the cars we drive, the way we comb our hair, or the problems we face. It is something essential, central, and something that we humans did not invent. It can never be claimed as "our own." It is God's and it is at the core of our being. If, with God's constant help, we can clear away enough of the junk in ourselves (and there is junk there), then perhaps the divine image may be uncovered, one day, to shine through every part of us.

God loves us because it is God's nature. What is the purpose of this love? Love, at its truest, is purposeless. It just is. Still, seen from our limited angle, we might speculate that perhaps it is for the sake of image that God loves us so, for the sake of this magnificent potential that God has given us. Perhaps it is because of the extreme difficulty of letting that potential become reality that God has such compassion on us. Clearing away the junk takes long, hard labor. But isn't the divine image worth the effort, the choice? Isn't God worth it?

In time, the outcome of refusing to tear myself down, of

letting myself accept my own nothingness *and* the inner presence of the divine image, is *gratitude* with self-acceptance. God has given me a chance to grow like young plants grow toward the sun. I may struggle to uncover this reflected image in me, if I choose to. What an opportunity! To become transparent as a clean windowpane, so that the image of God may shine unhindered through me, back toward God. That is the greatest opportunity in the universe. God in Christ Jesus opened it to me and to you. Good news indeed! How generous are God's gifts. How compassionate God's heart.

Saint Teresa of Avila had a healthy attitude. She knew she was nothing before God, but that God showered her with life and all its gifts. She knew she was not worthy of attention, but that God gave her love. And so she made great efforts to become what God wanted her to be. When she did something that was not so good or loving, she would say, "Well, Lord, what do you expect of anyone so ordinary as me?"

To sum up, today I can heartily and gratefully say, "I am nothing before God and unworthy of God's love. Yet I am just as worthy as any other person to live and grow, to receive love on earth. No one can earn God, but God invites me to union with compassion. God bestows dignity upon me and upon you. So I rejoice, for I am loved. Being loved creates the healthy, warm feeling of being worth something, as long as I remember my total dependence on God."

Here are steps for lessening our feelings of worthlessness while increasing the awareness of our nothingness before God's constant love.

- *Be as quiet as possible, either alone or with a friend.*
- *Look at your feelings of worthlessness.* You may want to explore within yourself for their beginnings. Or it may be enough just to learn how they work in you now.

- *Look for the distortion in your emotion of worthlessness:* whatever reflects a sense of your being less worthy than other people to live and grow and love. This worthless feeling is skewed and destructive to your life.
- *Look for the reflection of truth in your feeling:* whatever reflects your complete dependence on God, whatever helps you to know that it is God's very breath that keeps you alive, whatever reminds you of God's constant love for you. At first, this may seem difficult, but awareness of unworthiness is a hint of truth at this deeper level.
- *Accept the facts.* You are an imperfect creature, dependent on God's loving sustenance. Part of you is messed up and part of you is lovely. So join the human race—not a bad club to belong to. God loves it!
- *Relax!* God offers himself to all, you included. God offers gifts to all, you included. He makes everyone worthy to receive, you included. Other people offer love to you too. So relax, open your heart and receive God's compassion and the appreciation of others.
- *Laugh at yourself.* Marriage can really help a lot here. My husband and I are so different, sometimes one of us can't imagine how the other survives, doing things "so differently from each other!" He mirrors my silliness and I mirror his, just by being who we are. And it's odd but real: when I laugh at myself, I feel more worthy!

## Suggestions for Prayer

Use these words as a springboard for your own prayer:

*God of mercy, I know I am nothing before you. I am not separate or independent. I cannot even breathe on my own. So worthi-*

*ness in me is your creation. You made me to reflect yourself in this world. That is the source of my dignity. Please draw me close to you so that I may know your love. Show me how to open myself to others' love too. Teach me how to be more and more what you designed me to be. Thank you very much for the opportunities you give me.*

*Thank you that I am not alone in my littleness nor in my worth. Thank you for the other people who also are created in your image and who also are reflections of you. None of us are worthy of you; yet you love us all.*

## Scripture Suggestions

*Psalm 139:1-4*
O LORD, you have searched me and known me.
You know when I sit down and when I rise up;
   you discern my thoughts from far away.
You search out my path and my lying down,
   and are acquainted with all my ways.
Even before a word is on my tongue,
   O LORD, you know it completely.

*Ecclesiastes 3:10-13*
I have seen the business that God has given to everyone to be busy with. He has made everything suitable for its time; moreover he has put a sense of past and future into their minds, yet they cannot find out what God has done from the beginning to the end. I know that there is nothing better for them than to be happy and enjoy themselves as long as they live; moreover, it is God's gift that all should eat and drink and take pleasure in all their toil.

*Isaiah 49:15-16*
Can a woman forget her nursing child,
  or show no compassion for the child of her womb?
Even these may forget,
  yet I will not forget you.
See, I have inscribed you on the palms of my hands;
  your walls are continually before me.

*Romans 7:15-17*
I do not understand my own actions. For I do not do what I want, but I do the very thing I hate. Now if I do what I do not want, I agree that the law is good. But in fact it is no longer I that do it, but sin that dwells within me.

Here are some other Scripture references for reflection:

| | | |
|---|---|---|
| *Genesis 1:26-27,31* | *Isaiah 43:1-4* | *Luke 1:46-55* |
| *Psalm 8* | *Matthew 18:1-4* | *1 John 3:1-3* |

## For Reflection

Inventory your responses to the following topics:

- Have you ever felt inferior or unworthy?
- Have you gotten over it? How did you achieve that result? What facilitated such change?
- Consider which of the steps listed on pages 61-62 is the easiest for you. Begin there and share your experience with a friend or spiritual companion.
- Consider which of the steps listed at the end of the chapter will be the hardest for you. Reflect on these "hard" steps and explore ways in which you can take these steps.

# $\mathcal{C}$HAPTER $\mathcal{S}$IX

# FACE AND TRACE
# YOUR GUILT

*Forgiveness is one of the tools through which you can*
*empower your life to cause miracles to happen. The person*
*you have to forgive is yourself.*
TERRY COLE-WHITTAKER

*Guilt involves a sense of importance in the drama.*
*To say that one is not guilty is also to acknowledge*
*that one is in fact quite powerless.*
ELAINE PAGELS

Have you ever heard the expression "paralyzed by guilt"? I actually witnessed such paralysis one Sunday when I was resident manager of a halfway house for recovering mental patients.

I'll call her Bertha. She was yelling for me to come and help her. I went to her bedside, for she hadn't gotten up yet on this morning. "I can't move my legs," she was screaming.

I looked at her legs. As far as I could see, they were no different from the day before, when she'd been perfectly fine.

I was no doctor, but I knew that emotions could do dramatic things to bodies. I couldn't help her. Her physician came and he could find no cause. When I called her psychiatrist, he thought a moment, then said, "Call a priest. Bertha is Catholic."

So a priest came over. I was not in the room to hear them, but after he left, she walked into my room to show me she was okay. I asked her what happened and she simply said, "Father forgave me for taking too many pills."

No, she was not pretending all along. She *had* taken too many pills—over and over again. She also was extremely unstable emotionally. The point here is that her guilt feelings about the pills had, in fact, paralyzed her. Although most of us will never experience it so dramatically or so physically, we, too, can be immobilized, crippled, or held back by feelings of guilt if we choose to keep them. As with so many other attitudes, the choice is ours.

If guilt can cripple our lives, however, it can also be a strong incentive to get to know ourselves better and to make peaceful changes in our living. Let's take a positive look at those possibilities.

There seem to be several kinds of guilt feelings that we all experience at one time or another. One kind of guilt, most obviously, follows our having done something wrong, something hurtful to another person, something which violates our own values. When acts or decisions are morally unacceptable to us, we feel guilty. This kind of guilt flashes a warning signal: "Hey, something has gone wrong here!"

When I was in college, prevailing opinion seemed to assert that guilt was harmful and that it had better be gotten rid of or ignored. It was regarded as unhealthy to feel guilty about anything. But my wise religious studies professor, Dr. Tim Rieman, held that "When we feel guilty it's usually because we have done something we shouldn't have!" It was a refreshingly straightforward view. He was saying that guilt often had a reasonable and real cause. It could even be a useful feeling, evidence of our being in touch with reality at a necessary level of awareness.

Guilt for wrong-doing is healthy. It is a sign that our conscience is working.

Sometimes wrongs create an acute and unmistakable kind of guilt that is better called remorse. There is nothing vague about remorse. It cuts the heart like a sword. It burns the soul like a focused flame.

Once over the telephone, a man whom I respected totally, and who had mentored me most generously, asked me a question about myself. Instantly I knew that his opinion of me would be influenced by my answer. Before another thought could enter, the lie was out of my mouth. I didn't think about it again until I was driving along a freeway by myself. Then, suddenly, the lie shouted at me. My heart felt as if it were on fire. I couldn't even ask myself how I could have been so stupid. The remorse dominated all my feelings. Thanks to previous training, I knew to allow this fire to burn itself out, to purify my being of my wrong.

Remorse is no vague sense of guiltiness. Nor does it last a long time, if it is faced. It sears away the impure impulse that caused the wrong. One is not likely to repeat the fault. Because remorse over a definite wrong is so sharp and so active, we are not likely to cling to it as we may to other forms of guilt.

A second kind of guilt arises from violating self-adopted or self-invented standards. A friend once told me I was sick with a terrible case of "should-itis." I laughed, but his remark stayed with me and proved to be true. I feel I *should* always be capable; I *should* already know the answer; I *should* never make a mistake; I *should* use every moment of time productively; I *should* never be late; I *should* never express certain feelings; I *should* be able to do everything I read about; I *should*—well, my list is long.

Because many of these "should" standards—both yours and mine—are impossible, we suffer from chronic guilt. Vague, usually, but there. It can get pretty ridiculous, like feeling guilty over an extra ten minutes of morning rest.

Where do we get our should-itis? Some of these "shoulds" come from childhood, from parents or authorities in Church and school. Some of those early injunctions may well have been needed when we were children, but are hardly appropriate to adult life. Other "shoulds" are found in books, in stories about saints or in articles on psychological health. Others are self-invented, and these tend to be the silliest of all. The result: we feel guilty senselessly and unnecessarily. This kind of guilt can be frighteningly crippling.

Underlying much of our guilt that is related to unrealistic or inappropriate standards is a need to be right. To want to be right all the time can be a kind of pride, but it can also be a defense against a deep feeling that we are always wrong! For many, the need to be right is rooted in the feeling that only when we are right can we be loved. In relation to God, that is a horrible misunderstanding (though some parents have left that impression). God always loves us. God's love has nothing to do with our "rightness." Our ability to accept God's love may be affected, however, if we think we must always be right—who can ever be right all the time?

Our "oh, but I *should*" guilt can be chronic and have no recognizable reason. Some children have grown up under conditions that have left them always feeling guilty. When these children are adults, they still feel guilty, even in their dreams. They find no connections to anything they think or anything they do. They may experience themselves as guilty for even existing. These people do well to choose to get some psychological help, to heal those childhood misperceptions of themselves.

A third kind of guilt is, I believe, universal. Everybody has it. Universal guilt is subtle—and deep. It runs like an underground stream beneath our living, and only sometimes does it surface into conscious feeling. Universal guilt comes from that deep, inner part of us that knows that we have somehow separated ourselves from God. We are not living in the close intimacy with God that we were created to experience. We are involved in the human difficulty that we call sin.

We are made for God. More often than not, we are not aware of our life in God. Therefore, we are not the full human beings we were created to be. The resulting affliction is underlying guilt. It is with us all the time, until we learn a better way of relating to our own nature and to God.

Such guilt is sometimes fought by psychologists as being unhealthy. I do not agree with them. Nevertheless, to transform our underlying guilt into a source of goodness, effort is required. I think this effort can best be exerted along the lines discussed in the previous chapter on unworthiness.

What do we do with our guilt feelings? Some people cling to their guilt. They'd rather keep it than face the cause of guilt. Indeed, if we have done wrong, it's not easy to admit it to ourselves or to God. It can be much easier—or so we imagine—simply to go on feeling guilty. Usually those who choose to bury their guilt in this way are endangering their health, both physical and emotional. As with other fears, when we are afraid to face our wrongs or our violated standards, the best thing we can do for ourselves is to choose to look directly at the cause. Seeing is freeing.

Another reason some people cling to guilt is that it seems to them that they feel less vulnerable when they feel guilty than they do when they have to admit to wrongs. Living with the guilt is somehow preferable to living with the possibility that they can be mistaken, perhaps seriously so. When reflecting on it, though, doesn't it seem that the openness of vulnerability is a preferable experience to the miseries of guilt?

Some people choose guilt as an excuse for not changing themselves. How often have you heard—or said—"I know I should, *but*...and I feel so guilty"? After this statement comes: *no action*. One allows oneself to go on with the bad habit if one feels guilty enough—almost as if the guilt compensated for irresponsibility.

Choosing guilt over change is an evasion of responsibility for one's own experience. It is destructive. Nothing can be done to heal guilt and bring peace until one is ready to see its causes and take action to make tomorrow different. Guilt cries out for change!

In that, there is hope. If we acknowledge that we did something to get ourselves into this bind, then we can help ourselves get out again. If we feel guilty for an act or a habit, then, with help, we can alter that. The quality of our lives will improve. We will be freer and more peaceful if we look regularly at our guilt feelings, their roots, and then do something about our own condition.

How can we choose to let guilt warn us and then let it go? How can we choose to experience a life free of kept and chronic guilt feelings?

First, we practice observing the guilt feelings. We want to see how they operate inside us, what function they have for us. Do they hold us captive in an unwanted pattern? Do they affect our present choices? We need to be interested in our guilt—it will tell us a lot about ourselves if we listen carefully.

Frances Vaughan is a transpersonal psychologist. She advocates a mature life of responsible choice as best for all. She said to us in a workshop that one effective way to begin to make choices in the area of guilt is to make a list of our "shoulds." She's right. I call it "face it and trace it." It is done best when it is done prayerfully; we also see more clearly then. We face our guilty feeling and call that feeling by its name. Whether our guilt feelings are from violated standards or real wrongs, we need to know how they arose.

So we trace the guilt to its cause. When the cause is clear, we can determine what kind of guilt we are feeling. Is it due to a real wrong-doing? Or have we violated some private standard? Or do we feel guilty because we aren't as profoundly intimate with God as we could be? Is it, "Mom said…" or "The book says…" or "I think…" or "I know I should, *but* …"?

If our guilt is really remorse, we will know the difference without a moment's thought. Remorse, as we have already seen, burns with an unmistakable fire. If we allow it to burn in our hearts, it will bring itself to completion. There is nothing we need to do about it except allow it to do its purifying work inside ourselves.

Having faced our guilt feeling and traced it, we can begin to help ourselves.

First, think! Decide whether the reason for guilt is a real one that stems from a genuine wrong. Or have you just missed something or gotten tangled up in your own too-high standards? Did an accident occur? Did you make a simple mistake, then drive yourself into guilt over it? Does the cause of your guilt deserve more attention in your life?

If it is a principle of Christian life, then it is valuable. If our wrong is a real one, it's important to acknowledge that.

If the standard I'm measuring myself against is something

Dad told me when I was nine, it may not be valuable any-more. Then it's a symptom of should-itis. If it's a notion I inherited from my family, I can decide whether or not I want to keep it. If I abandon the standard, then I can let go of the guilt along with it. If the standard is a long-held one, it may take a while to let it go. Watching our speech and changing it to match our new choice can be a help. Talking with a friend about the inappropriate standard can help us *feel* its probable silliness.

For all kinds of guilt, confessing my wrongs—real or imag-ined—may be helpful. In admitting the nature of the wrong that I have committed, I take a step back from that ugliness within me. I admit that my better self does not want to hang on to my deed or to the tendencies that moved me to do it. Thus I create a little distance, a little space, between me and my wrong. If I feel remorse, the purifying flame creates an inner spaciousness. Into that space, the love of God can come. God is always ready for this space to open. His strength will help me not to repeat what I have now decided against. This is healing.

If the thing I'm admitting to is actually a moral wrong, then the value of this public acknowledgment is clear. When it isn't actually wrong but is a "should," I may declare this perceived wrong just the same. I also then admit the mis-taken standard—as something I've inflicted on myself un-necessarily. It, too, needs healing.

Sometimes I must admit to another trusted person my own vague guilt that seems to be just human. I confess that I don't live as close to God as I wish or that I don't live up to the spiritual potential I know is within me. Then the friend and I may agree that we don't know exactly what's happen-ing, but together we confirm my sorrow at feeling sepa-rated from God and affirm God's love for me.

The universal human sense of guilt can also remind me of my vulnerability. I am not able, by myself, to do or to become anything. I am vulnerable to God because I am so completely dependent on his mercy. The more aware I am of vulnerability, the more I love God for God's singular love of me, and the more God can help me to peace. *And* the less unhealthy guilt I carry over all my "shoulds."

These admissions to another human being imply a willingness to accept God's forgiveness. Accepting forgiveness is not always easy. Sometimes it is such a relief that we fall into it like grateful children into the arms of a loving parent. If, on the other hand, accepting forgiveness is difficult for you, consider this: is the difficulty that you always must be right before God? If so, that stance also is in need of forgiveness and change.

If you cannot emotionally accept forgiveness yet, then accept it in words and in your intention. Ask God to deepen your acceptance. Get to the root of your inability to accept forgiveness, and beg for God's grace to change you there. God will always help. And remember: God's grace is necessary to support any human desire. Before God, all of us are always beggars—beloved beggars indeed, but with nothing of our own.

Sometimes our inability to accept God's forgiveness is rooted in an unforgiveness in our own heart. If we are holding the slightest grudge, the smallest resentment against another person, we will not be able to accept the Lord's forgiveness of ourselves. Keeping anger against another acts like a block in our heart, and God's generous love cannot get past it. We must be willing to let go of all resentments if we want God to forgive us (see Matthew 6:14-15).

A helpful way to transform guilt feelings is to make reparation, even if it is about one of those unrealistic "shoulds."

We sometimes call this "making satisfaction." I don't know where that phrase came from, but it is deep-down satisfying to fix up something I have damaged. The need for reparation may be as clear as repaying stolen money. However, clarity is not always present. Sometimes we just know we need to repair a relationship or to patch up disruptions we've caused or to clear the habitual clutter from our life or from our prayer.

Sometimes the repair can be made directly. For example, I can go to the person involved, apologize, and try to undo the damage. At other times, the people I've hurt may also need time and sensitivity. They may not be able to respond directly. Then we seek indirect ways of making satisfaction. We must ask God for insight about this. When other people are not involved, we may make a frontal attack on one of our habitual faults. That restores our self-respect.

Sometimes repairing damage after a wrong can be the beginning of a whole new and lovely practice for life. Once I refused to give anything to a begging woman with a small, thin child in her arms. This woman will haunt me forever. But since that time, I no longer refuse help that is requested and I give as well when nothing is asked. My life is freer for this and the world is a teeny bit better too. The great guilt I felt over that early refusal to help has been transformed into new choices. They are loving. They are peace-giving.

The act of reparation can also be used symbolically. When I have disrupted life, I need to help restore the balance I have disturbed. The world has problems enough without me adding to them! But occasionally I do, so then I prefer to turn and help where I can. If I can't fix my own damage, I can always add to the world's store of goodness. If I can't unsay the ugly words I said, I can say other words that add love to the atmosphere. Today, Scriptures can be used to direct love to the world. That is needed.

Of course, the final answer to all guilt is the grateful acceptance of God's grace. I don't deserve it. Neither do you. We can never be good enough to deserve God's eternal compassion! We can know ourselves well enough to admit that we need God. We can open our hearts to receive him more. God's grace will do whatever secret things need to be done to heal our weaknesses if we want them healed. God will return us to loving relationship and will remove our ugliness when we cry with the psalmist, "Have mercy on me, O God…wash me thoroughly from my iniquity…cleanse me from my sin…create in me a clean heart" (Psalm 51:1,2,10).

Especially when our guilt feelings stem from the human condition we all experience, it is vital to call out to God and depend on grace. When all is done and we have given it our very best effort, we are still dependent on God's mercy. So why not begin depending actively on God for cleansing of guiltiness altogether? That is a way of self-knowledge and peace.

Along with our acceptance of Divine Compassion, our heart must open in gratitude to the Compassionate Giver. If we do not know the ecstasy of gratitude, we will never know the One who holds us so dearly and who so freely gives us the strength and forgiveness we need. When gratitude begins to flow in the heart, let it flow through the lips as well. Stay with it as long as possible, until your heart is light once again.

From facing and tracing our guilt feelings, choosing to do something different with our lives, and from gratefully accepting God's gracious forgiveness, we learn something new about life: life is not a demand. It is not a mysterious contract that we signed and can't remember except for its sense of obligation. Life is a gift. Gifts are not occasions for guilt. They are occasions for shared joy and happy responses.

Life, too, offers us ever new possibilities for joyfulness. Life offers the opportunity for happiness that springs from the heart, where dwells our loving God. If we block this gift by seeing it as demand, we will always feel guilty. If we accept this gift with delight, our guilt will warn us when needed and then fade quickly away. Peace will be ours.

Here is a summary of the steps that may help you achieve freedom from guilt. Take these steps with much prayer:

- *Face your guilt feelings, and observe their operation within you.*
- *Name the kind of guilt you are experiencing.*
- *Trace the guilt to its real cause.*
- *Evaluate the cause, and choose whether or not to keep the measuring stick you are using.*
- *Admit your guilt and its cause to at least one other trusted person, and be open to healing.*
- *Make reparation. Repair the damage or do the penance or speak the healing words. Add extra goodness to your corner of the world.*
- *Accept God's forgiveness with gratitude.*
- *Begin to depend consciously on the ongoing grace and mercy of God to strengthen your choices and free you from all guilt.*

## Suggestions for Prayer

When praying about guilt, the best prayer is one that acknowledges the wrong or the felt-wrong or the sorry state of one's life and nature. Such prayer opens the heart for God who always wants to heal us and welcome us.

Please don't tear yourself down before God, any more than you would beat up someone else before God. Be respectful of yourself and be honest with God.

When the purge of your wrongs is completed, make some formal acceptance of God's forgiveness and love.

Then just rest quietly a while. Turn your attention to God's great understanding of you, his great love for you. Be still and listen for God's response. Allow God's love to penetrate your defensiveness. Remain quietly attentive until you know within yourself that it is completed. Then offer your thanks to God and go about your activities in peace.

## Scripture Suggestions

*Psalm 51:1-2*
Have mercy on me, O God,
  according to your steadfast love;
according to your abundant mercy
  blot out my transgressions.
Wash me thoroughly from my iniquity,
  and cleanse me from my sin.

*Proverbs 28:13*
No one who conceals transgressions will prosper,
but one who confesses and forsakes them will obtain mercy.

*Isaiah 57:16-18*
For I will not continually accuse,
  nor will I always be angry;
for then the spirits would grow faint before me,
  even the souls that I have made.
Because of their wicked covetousness I was angry;
  I struck them, I hid and was angry;
  but they kept turning back to their own ways.
I have seen their ways, but I will heal them;

> I will lead them and repay them with comfort,
> creating for their mourners the fruit of the lips.

*1 John 1:8-9*
If we say that we have no sin, we deceive ourselves, and the truth is not in us. If we confess our sins, he who is faithful and just will forgive us our sins and cleanse us from all unrighteousness.

Here are some Scripture references for reflection:

*Exodus 34:6*      *Hosea 14:2-3,5-7*      *Matthew 5:23-26*
*Numbers 5:5-8*    *Ephesians 1:3-8*       *James 5:16*
*Psalm 86:11-16*

## For Reflection

Guilt can be a heavy topic with which to deal alone, so go slowly and with great compassion for yourself. On a sheet of paper list five things for which you feel guilty. Then write "I forgive myself for_____, I forgive myself for_____, I forgive myself for_____," and so on.

Set the paper aside. Look at the list again the next day. Add more things that have come to mind, and again write forgiveness for yourself for each new item on your list.

Set the paper aside again, and look at it on the third day, adding further instances if necessary. Write out your forgiveness for yourself for each of these items. Then burn or destroy the list on the third day with an attitude of compassion for yourself and all those involved on the list.

## CHAPTER SEVEN

# BREAK YOUR LONELINESS HABIT

*It is ironic that the one thing that
all religions recognize as separating us
from our creator—our very self-consciousness—
is also the one thing that divides us
from our fellow creatures.*
ANNIE DILLARD

*Loneliness and the feeling of being unwanted
is the most terrible poverty.*
MOTHER TERESA

Loneliness. The very word casts frightening shadows on our hearts. All of us have experienced it. All of us are likely to believe that we have never chosen loneliness. All of us may feel that in this at least we are certainly victims. We are lonely because other people do not call, others do not invite us to them, others do not share with us. Surely it is the actions of other people that bring on our loneliness.

When I accepted the basic principle that I bore the chief responsibility for all of my emotional life, I also had to look at the loneliness I felt. I wanted a closer life with people, or so I thought, and it was hard for me to find my own accountability here. I did have friends, but I wanted contact with a wider variety of people. I wished for friendship with a few specific people whom I admired. I wanted a mutually affectionate social life with others.

Thinking about it, I knew that I already understood a good deal about promoting friendships. So perhaps I had unrecognized habits that did not help new friendships arise and flourish. Again, the first place to look was within myself; but I also wanted to observe the way I acted with other people. As I'd already learned from my work with other emotions, I first needed to know how I felt and behaved.

This time it didn't take long to see, but my ego shrank before my discoveries: I didn't make full use of small talk as a means of simple, gentle sharing with other people. In casual gatherings, such as meeting people on street corners, I was almost always the first to leave. I sometimes treated people's sharing as a problem to be solved rather than as a slice of life to be respected and savored. There were other habits too. These were only the first I saw. I wasn't pleased with myself. I had, however, discovered definite behaviors that I could change right away.

So I went to work on these habits, gradually but definitely choosing other ways of acting. I learned small talk about the merest trifles, just so I could be with someone. Then I found it wasn't so hard to move into more interesting things, especially about the other person. When I met people unexpectedly, I glued my feet down, even though I had nothing to say and felt uncomfortable. I stayed until at least one other person had gone. I began to practice responding to people's feelings rather than trying to solve their problems. I learned that those two go well together. As I worked at these changes, a curious and unexpected trait showed up: I could be playful, even funny! When I choose to be responsible, the most delightful surprises bubbled up from inside!

Gradually, openings for deeper sharing and broader experiences came of themselves. I have sometimes wondered if anyone really noticed the changes. Perhaps, but I doubt it. I think people just naturally responded with appreciation to their experience of me and didn't realize that I was changing myself. If these changes had taken place in a close-knit family, the transformation might have been noticed more. But it doesn't matter whether or not others are aware of this growth. They will respond to these changes anyway. So gradually I experienced less isolation when I began to accept responsibility for my own loneliness and to change habits that had helped cause it.

There are probably as many loneliness-producing habits as there are people. You will be able to find your own if you look. A common one is the habit of not sharing our own real feelings, our real hopes and sadness, our real selves. Of course, that deeper sharing is risky. It's possible that another person will not understand or will not care. Perhaps it's best to explore gradually how much to share. You may not want to open your deepest secrets to everyone. But a bit of our real selves can always be offered to another. If it is received with kindness, then it is fine to share more.

Little by little, as we practice, we also grow in strength. Then we can share ourselves whether people like it or not. It's interesting, however, to find that they almost always do!

Our sharing of our real selves is linked to listening to the real self of the other person and appreciating the private beauties offered to us. Then each person has a chance to listen with love and to share with enthusiasm. Few relationships are perfectly mutual at all times. But most friendships do include this deeper, two-sided sharing called intimacy. As intimacy increases, it grows into a close, safe assurance and an endearing knowledge of each other. If even one friendship (in or outside the family) has this quality, our loneliness is much decreased. It is well worth seeking and fostering such a friendship.

Intimate life-sharing carries over into those times when we may actually be alone. It brings warmth and enjoyment of living even when we are distant from the person whom we know and love so well. We may wish he or she were with us, but we do not experience the empty, hurtful isolation that comes when we have no intimate human relationships. So, building intimacy by sharing and listening is a fruitful way to respond to loneliness.

Even so, there will be times when we are alone or feel lonely. If these times make up most of our life, then our relationships clearly need to be worked on.

But if we already have the basic loving support of friends, then loneliness can bring a special opportunity. We can turn our loneliness into solitude. Instead of feeling lonely by victimization, we can feel solitary by choice. In solitude there is vast peacefulness. When chosen, it allows our souls to expand as wide as the sky, as broad as the ocean. Solitude is quiet, nearly silent, making us want to tiptoe through the vastness of our own inner spirit.

Many people complain that they don't have enough time for themselves. They are too busy. Moments of loneliness can be turned into solitude, giving the deep and quieting inner stretch that brings us serenity.

These snatches of solitude may be only moments: when the kids have roared away from the house, when someone is in the hospital, when friends have just left, when I awake in the morning before a word is spoken, or when I feel lonely for no apparent reason at all.

It's hard to describe the lovely inward quality that we create when we turn loneliness into solitude, but here are suggestions for your own exploration of that shift. You will make your own discoveries.

- *Accept your lonely feelings.* It is okay to feel lonely at times. If you feel lonely all the time, give yourself and your relationships the attentive examination I have described. Find your unwanted habits and begin to change them.
- *Quiet yourself.* Sit or lie comfortably, turn off all distractions, both outside and within. If you can look at nature (sky or sea or forest or plain), do so. If not, imagine a favorite scene in your mind; feel yourself actually present there. You may want to use recordings of nature sounds (birds, ocean waves, rain) that are available.
- *If emotions surface, let them flow, let them be.* Watch them as you might watch a river, until they have flowed through you and on past.
- *When your attention wanders, bring it back slowly and gently.* Reestablish your attention to the view or your image or the quiet that is pervading you. Simply be with what is.
- *Let the stillness embrace you.* Let it touch you deep within. Gently hold yourself absolutely still, as if you were listening to identify a sound. Let your lips smile a little.

## Suggestions for Prayer

Since we have deep within our being a genuine and permanent loneliness for God, it is to be expected that it will surface to our awareness at times. We might mistake it for some other kind of loneliness. When we turn any loneliness into solitude, we can also fill it with the intimacy of prayer. Silence is the perfect prayer, full of loving, attentive listening, just being open to God in whatever way God is. We can silently allow God to see all that we are, wordlessly sharing our deepest self. Thus we are drawn closer to God's heart. We can listen intimately to God, too, when we are this quiet and this open.

So, when you have reflected through the five steps above, turn your attention softly to God and wait for God in the silence. God is there already, waiting for you.

## Scripture Suggestions

*Proverbs 18:19-21*
An ally offended is stronger than a city;
    such quarreling is like the bars of a castle.
From the fruit of the mouth one's stomach is satisfied;
    the yield of the lips brings satisfaction.
Death and life are in the power of the tongue,
    and those who love it will eat its fruits.

*Sirach 6:5-6; 14-17*
Pleasant speech multiplies friends,
    and a gracious tongue multiplies courtesies.
Let those who are friendly with you be many,
    but let your advisers be one in a thousand.

Faithful friends are a sturdy shelter;
  whoever finds one has found a treasure.
Faithful friends are beyond price;
  no amount can balance their worth.
Faithful friends are life-saving medicine;
  and those who fear the Lord will find them.
Those who fear the Lord direct their friendship aright,
  for as they are, so are their neighbors also.

*Sirach 9:10*
Do not abandon old friends,
  for new ones cannot equal them.
A new friend is like new wine;
  when it has aged, you can drink it with pleasure.

*Colossians 3:12-15*
As God's chosen ones, holy and beloved, clothe yourselves
with compassion, kindness, humility, meekness, and pa-
tience. Bear with one another and, if anyone has a complaint against another, forgive each other; just as the Lord
has forgiven you, so you also must forgive. Above all, clothe
yourselves with love, which binds everything together in
perfect harmony. And let the peace of Christ rule in your
hearts, to which indeed you were called in the one body.
And be thankful.

  Here are some additional Scripture references for reflection:

*1 Samuel 18:1-3*     *Sirach 22:19-26*     *John 21:20-22*
*Psalm 22*            *John 15:14-17*       *Psalm 23*
*Psalm 42:1-66*

## For Reflection

Ask yourself these questions as a start toward healing the hurts of loneliness.

- Have I always assumed that loneliness was caused by other people's reactions to me?
- How fully do I recognize that loneliness involves my own choices?
- When have I felt most lonely?
- When have I felt least lonely?
- What have I done to decrease my loneliness? Did it work?
- How have I chosen solitude?

$\mathcal{C}$HAPTER $\mathcal{E}$IGHT

# FIND HIDDEN GIFTS
# IN DISAPPOINTMENT

*The greater part of our happiness or misery depends*
*on our dispositions and not on our circumstances.*
MARTHA WASHINGTON

*There is the greatest practical benefit*
*in making a few failures early in life.*
T. H. HUXLEY

*When we long for life without difficulties,*
*remind us that oaks grow strong in contrary winds*
*and diamonds are made under pressure.*
PETER MARSHALL

Within my mind is a picture gallery. Many treasures hang there. Most of them are quite lovely, or at least I think they are. A few are not lovely at all, but they have senti-mental value. Many of the pictures I have painted myself, some quickly and others slowly and carefully. Still others have been painted by people around me or by the TV or by books. But only one person has ever been in charge of deciding which pictures are hung in this gallery: me. I spend quite a bit of time there. I enjoy the pictures. I want to keep them.

Sometimes an everyday event knocks one or more of these pictures askew or smashes it on the floor. When that happens, a lot of emotion wells up in me. It's unpleasant, maybe even miserable. That emotion is called disappointment. You see, I want life to go according to the pictures I've chosen. They all seem so good and reasonable. However, other people don't even know about my private gallery, and they certainly wouldn't feel bound by my choices because they have galleries of their own. So the realities of living often do not match the pictures in my gallery. At such a moment, I'm likely to feel disappointed.

Disappointment has a special sound all its own: "But I wanted it so much!" Or "But I was really looking forward to that." Or "But I've dreamed of that all my life!" Or "But I counted on that." Or "But I was so sure it would…"

What the sound of disappointment and the fallen picture have in common is smashed expectation. When what is expected doesn't become a reality, disappointment results. As I review the disappointments in my life, some of them now appear mild and not too important; others were devastating, and overwhelmed me for a long time. But big or little, they all were the result of expectations (and wishes) that did not work out the way I thought they would.

If we hear the sound of disappointment in a child's voice, we know that explanation and comfort are needed because the child is feeling hurt and upset. We would do well to be equally as kind to ourselves. When we feel disappointed, we need to explain to ourselves just what our expectations were and why they didn't come to completion. (This may be harder than explaining to children.) We deserve some comfort too. We may ask for an extra hug, call a friend and complain loudly, eat a piece of chocolate, huddle before a warm fire. It helps to provide comfort for ourselves when disappointment comes.

For a child, comfort from a loving parent may be all that is needed. For adults, however, increased self-understanding is also necessary.

If I am responsible for the quality of my life, I play a part in my own disappointment. I am the one who builds up the expectations. I am the one who is attached to them. If my attachment is great, as when two people are engaged and making wonderful future plans, the disappointment can be just as great. If my attachment is small, as when I expect to make onion soup and find no onions in the house, the disappointment won't be so acute. The important thing to notice is that the intensity of attachment I have to my expectations varies. That means it can be changed by my own attention and effort.

Even in the greatest disappointments I have experienced, I have found that when I get a clear view of the expectations, some of the sting goes out of the comedown. Part of that sting seems to come from a feeling of helplessness—of not being able to make things happen as I expected. It is easy enough to feel like a victim then. But when I see the large contribution my own hopes made to the intensity of my disappointment, I can accept responsibility for it; my feeling of helplessness is lessened. Yes, I still must live with the circumstances as they are; but I will know that I'm not helpless in regard to my feelings, that the expectations I created were not my very self. The beauties of life remain open to me—in other forms than I had anticipated.

This does not imply that all expectations can be eliminated. They help us function well, especially in making decisions. Still, our expectancies can be held a little more loosely. I still paint pictures for my gallery, but now, after years of life, I know that some of them will fall. So I don't attach them as firmly when I hang them up!

It's our choice. We can learn to say to ourselves, "I'd love it if it would turn out like this…(here paint in your details); but if it doesn't, there will be other opportunities." For those who decide to do this, pictures may be cherished; but they are loved as possibilities or as guidelines for action. They are no longer required for our "survival" or happiness. We are no longer devastated when our gallery pictures tumble.

When disappointment does come, we don't need to pretend that we feel "just fine" about it. We can examine our expectations and see exactly what happened inside ourselves to bring on the disappointment. Then we may choose to let go of those expectations and to concentrate instead on what really did happen.

When I practice this choice, it brings an unexpected bonus: a small, exquisite sense of wonder begins to seep into my heart—wonder at what *did* happen. Very often when things don't turn out as I plan, there is a quiet "wow" within, as I ponder what life offers me. I don't always like it right away. But I can always seek the hidden gift that all the new circumstances offer, even when it takes a long time to uncover it.

Letting go of old expectations is a way of living in the present moment, of drawing myself together right here, right now. When I look at *now*, there is always something okay within me and with the circumstances. I may be able to feel gratitude for all the knowns and unknowns that have brought me to this moment. I may find a precious poignancy in the disappointment that spreads gently to soften my heart. I may see a new beauty around me. I may want to take this moment, with all my feelings (without the expectations), and hold it lovingly in my cupped hands as I might hold a soft baby chick.

When I give myself to the present, life *as it is* becomes my treasure. It's a real treasure, not a make-believe one that I painted myself and hung in my head. In fact, I noticed something interesting the last time I strolled through my gallery. There weren't as many pictures as there used to be! There were a lot of blank spaces. Since I've begun loosening the grip on my expectations and enjoying the present, I feel less interest in expectations. The present is so full of remarkable things to appreciate: feelings, events, challenges, wonders.

So, these days, instead of trying to make happenings fit the pictures in my head, I am open to experiencing the day's events with anticipation. Oh, without a doubt I will feel disappointment again at times, for my gallery is not empty. But in between those ever-rarer times, I am busy storing lovely memories in my gallery instead.

I believe, too, that treasuring what is real leads us closer to God. God is the most real, the only Real. If I habitually look only for the match to my own idea of how things should be, I can miss the Real Wonder that God is. My own expectations can blind me. It happened to many of the Jewish leaders at the time of Jesus. They had expected the Messiah for centuries. Furthermore, they cherished very clear pictures of what he would be like and what he would do. But when Jesus came, they couldn't see who he was because their expectations muddied their vision. Something similar has happened to me, too, and has kept me from seeing and accepting the magnificent gifts that God offered me. I do not wish that to happen again.

Here are steps for practice and exploration. In some ways, I think expectations are among the most private parts of ourselves, so you may find that other steps work better for you than these. If so, use them. Share them too.

- *When you are feeling disappointed, take a moment to name your expectations.* Examine them with care and learn how they brought you to your upset feelings.
- *Lay aside those expectations for a minute.* Look at the present moment. Is it, in itself, really unbearable? Are you in serious danger? Are you destroyed? Is there anything wrong with *this moment* that does *not* have to do with your expectations? What is there in this moment that is good and fine?
- *Ask yourself, "What can this moment's reality offer to my future?"* What quality does it bring into your life? What aspect of this situation is actually a new opportunity?
- *Choose what you want to do with your unfulfilled expectations.* You may want to let them go entirely. Or you may see a value in them that you want to keep, perhaps changing them to fit new circumstances or new possibilities.
- *When you have chosen, speak your choice aloud.* If you can take an immediate action to support your new choice, by all means act!
- *Enjoy the present moment.* Allow it—even cherish it—as it is. Too quickly it will go its way. Is there anything here you want to keep for your memory gallery? In the movie *Yentl*, a young girl experiences several events that are especially significant to her. They are not all pleasant, but each has a precious poignant beauty. Even in pain, she celebrates these unique, exquisite moments in song. It's a fine way to love life and let it love you back.

## Suggestions for Prayer

Jesus must have known many unfulfilled hopes in his public life. He lamented over Jerusalem and for its people who would not come to him. He sometimes grieved at the unresponsiveness and misunderstanding of his closest disciples. So when you feel disappointed, you can pour out your feelings to him. Tell Jesus exactly how it is—what you expected, how much you wanted it, how it turned out, and how hurt you feel. Let it all out to the Lord.

Then imitate those who wrote the psalms. Over and over they voiced their sorrows and fears, then in the next breath praised God for his goodness to them. They remembered what they knew: God is present, and God is utterly good and compassionate. You, too, can praise God for who he is, and praise God for the present as it is. Offer your moment of disappointment, with its emptiness and its fullness. God will renew your hope in the beauties of living and is infinitely able to turn your mourning into joy.

## Scripture Suggestions

*Psalm 86:1-2*
Incline your ear, O LORD, and answer me,
   for I am poor and needy.
Preserve my life, for I am devoted to you;
   save your servant who trusts in you.

*Joshua 1:9*
"I hereby command you: Be strong and courageous; do not be frightened or dismayed, for the LORD your God is with you wherever you go."

*1 Corinthians 15:57-58*
But thanks be to God, who gives us the victory through our Lord Jesus Christ. Therefore, my beloved, be steadfast, immovable, always excelling in the work of the Lord, because you know that in the Lord your labor is not in vain.

*James 1:12*
Blessed is anyone who endures temptation. Such a one has stood the test and will receive the crown of life that the Lord has promised to those who love him.

Here are additional Scripture references for reflection:

| | | |
|---|---|---|
| *Psalm 57* | *John 14:1-2* | *Psalm 77* |
| *Isaiah 40:28-31* | *Romans 8:35-39* | *Psalm 116* |
| | *James 4:13-15* | |

## *For Reflection*

Identify your responses to these questions.

- What are the most important pictures in the gallery of your life story?
- What have been your most obvious disappointments? What expectations led up to them?
- What expectations are you aware of in relation to your spouse? your children? your Church? your friends?
- Say aloud to yourself, "I think life should be…" and listen to your answers. Then listen to your feelings about these expectations.

# CHAPTER Nine

# KNOW YOUR
# LIMITATIONS

*Do what you can, with what you have, where you are.*
THEODORE ROOSEVELT

*Everything has its wonders, even darkness
and silence, and I learn, whatever state I may
be in, therein to be content.*
HELEN KELLER

Furiously, Kent was hammering words at me. "But *why* aren't you going to the party?"

"Because I'm scared."

That merely brought on a stream of strongly worded protests.

"Besides," I said, "I don't like what I know they will do there. And I feel uncertain and insecure about that kind of socializing."

More strong words from Kent.

But, as it turned out, Kent didn't care about the party. He was trying to get through to me about myself. He finally hollered, "Marilyn! Damn it! You are a powerful woman! You could turn that party into any sort of party you wanted—and do it easier than anybody who will be there. Stop running from your own gifts!"

It looks mild on paper, but Kent—all six feet of him—was yelling directly in my face.

It is, unfortunately, rare that anyone confronts me directly, so I listened. His anger translated easily into intense concern for me. I knew that he saw something in me that I had not seen or had not taken seriously. He did not want to see me waste that something. What was it?

He said I was powerful. Was I? If so, then why didn't I have the life I wanted? I started to tell myself why: "My childhood was so-and-so instead of thus-and-so; my early decisions were so-and-so instead of thus-and-so; I didn't have what I would have had if so-and-so; I did have other things I didn't want to have; if only…" Suddenly, the whole story didn't sound very convincing to me! Kent hadn't known any of it. He only saw something valuable that I didn't use. He saw that I was making a long list of excuses for my life. This time, when I told myself my sad story, I *heard* how thin and dubious it all sounded.

Was Kent correct? I decided to make a test case of the party. Could I turn it into the kind of experience I liked instead of assuming everyone else had all the controls? It was no surprise to Kent or to anyone else that I could—and did. It was a great surprise to me. I found a capacity to create circumstances with qualities that I chose! It was so intriguing that I began to explore it more.It was a long exploration. Some of its fruits appear in this book. But that party taught me one truth. I watched myself, listened to my friends, thought as honestly as I could about what I saw and heard. All the evidence confirmed my discovery: I had habitually focused on my limitations; I had been ignoring my powers, my gifts. I had gone around feeling sorry for myself and making excuses. (Here I must say that few others saw this in my life; Kent spotted it and his observation was accurate.)

When I looked around at other people, I acted from what Transactional Analysis calls a "one-down position." That means I assumed before I even breathed that everyone else knew more and was better than I. When I recognized my assumption, it was obvious that it was false. Everyone is not better, wiser, more powerful, more intelligent, more loving or more gifted than I. *Some* people are *some* of these things. Other people have less of one or more of these qualities.

When I compared myself to the top people in every field—religion, music, psychology, writing, money-making, or whatever—of course I was not their equal in their fields! It is crippling to look at these people if I then feel hopeless about myself in comparison. I needed to stop comparing myself to them in that way.

Yet great people could always teach me something useful. Think about these: Itzhak Perlman, unable to walk without crutches, but a master violinist! Fritz Künkel lost an arm during his medical training, yet became a great psychiatrist (whose writings were a major help to me); Catherine of Siena became a saint over the opposition of her huge family, as did Francis of Assisi; Robert Louis Stevenson wrote almost all of his wonderful stories while in bed with tuberculosis. There were those lesser-knowns too: the blind man who became a competitive fencer; the quadriplegic who painted with her brush in her mouth; the polio victim who became an athlete. Reflecting on these people, one thing stood out: they chose not to focus on their limitations, no matter how overwhelming. They chose to focus persistently on their capacities.

No one can do everything or be everybody! That is not what life—or God—presents to us. Rather, we are given the opportunity to *be fully* what we *can* be. For each of us, that is a lot. It is very much more than each of us is now. The people who make themselves beautiful are those who accept their limitations as facts, then devote themselves in a big way to the development of their powers, their talents, their abilities. They love their gifts, they want their real possibilities.

It is important to know our limitations. They will affect our lives in ways that cannot be seen. I do not regret the time and attention it took to accept my limitations, beginning with the fact that I was around forty instead of twenty-two! It strengthened me to learn the effects of those limitations. There was a good, solid reality in them. But once I was acquainted with these aspects of myself, I practiced turning my attention to the other side, the side of possibilities and gifts.

That side, too, I needed to discover and to understand. It was, oddly, harder to look at my gifts than my limitations. That may have been because it was an unfamiliar view or, perhaps, because I knew I would then be responsible for the use and development of the gifts I saw.

Limitations were not really the source of my difficulties. I had gifts, more than I thought when I started looking. I got stuck not by limitations or lack of gifts, but by focusing wrongly, plus not choosing carefully which gifts to develop.

Career was not the main issue for me. I was seeking a quality of living, an inner capacity to be the fullest person I could be. I wanted to feel effective as a human being, to express my particular character, to feel confidence in my whole self. No doubt, when I lovingly followed after my gifts, a career might develop too. But it was basically quality that I wanted, quality for every day and quality of accomplishment.

Measured in years, my life was far along. How much could I reach at this late date? Certainly, I could not develop all my gifts to the maximum *imaginable* point. But I could choose the possibilities I enjoyed the most, the ones that expressed my deeper desires. No one was demanding anything in particular. Not even God had grabbed me by the collar and insisted! He had, instead, given me several possibilities, but it seemed the choices were up to me.

So, ever so slowly—I think I'm the eternal slow learner—I began to observe myself to see which of my possibilities I liked the best. I chose to love them, nurture them, develop them. I began gradually to grow toward what Abraham Maslow calls a "self-actualized" person. By that he means one whose life works in ways that are strong, healthy, creative; a person who makes her own decisions and follows them through; a person who, to the stranger, may seem unlimited and who influences life around her.

Experimenting, I found that I couldn't grab immediately the qualities I wanted. I couldn't get up in the morning and say, "Now today I will be wise." Or "This afternoon is my time to be creative." Qualities seemed to be by-products of other choices, other efforts. The search for quality, however, can be a constant endeavor. There are practices I can undertake to establish the inner environment that encourages quality to emerge.

The following steps are partly my own discoveries and are influenced by Maslow. I assure you that I practice them and they work for me. They can work for you too.

- *Resolve to be especially honest in this investigation of yourself.* You will only waste your time if you are not.
- *Review your limitations and notice how they work.* Do this with a light touch and do not use your limitations as excuses. Your sad story may hurt, but it is only one in a million sad stories. The most it can do for you is push you to choose a better quality for the rest of your life.
- *Accept your limitations as facts.* Don't dwell on them. They will probably stay with you, but they are already only a small part of you. As your other qualities expand, the proportion of limitations will get smaller.
- *Turn your attention and your interest to your gifts, your possibilities.* I was so unskilled at this that I had to go to friends and teachers and ask them what gifts they saw, why they valued me, what they liked in me. Their reflections were astounding to me, but turned out to be quite reliable. They gave me a place to begin a new aspect of self-knowledge.
- *Listen to yourself.* What do you like? What do you choose over and over? What is fun? What gives you joy? What do you find interesting? What do you want from your heart? Explore these preferences. Get to know them. Give them time and effort. Nurture them. They are important keys to the person you can be. They are clues to the qualities you have already, waiting to be expressed in your life.
- *Whatever you are doing, especially if you have chosen it, care about quality.* The attitude "that's good enough to get by" may bring results if you are talented, but it is not enough to develop your own personal power. It doesn't help your growth much. Give your choices careful attention, love, time, effort. Be generous enough with yourself to be good at it—whatever "it" is.

My husband once learned to make an apple pie. It was an education to watch him. Every detail was slowly, caringly done. He skipped nothing, hurried nothing. He savored every move, gave every slice of apple, every bit of crust, his whole attention. When the pie came out of the oven, he held it up on his fingertips and exclaimed, "Now *that* is a work of art!" It was. He knows the secret of quality work and the joy it brings.

- *Cherish every moment of beauty that comes your way.* Whether you created this beauty or it came from else-where, if you like this loveliness, if it feels satisfying, bask in it. If you see a sunset, feast your eyes and your soul on it. If you enjoy the embrace of a loved one, melt into it. If someone brings you a flower, notice every detail and marvel. Every precious thing, small and large, is to be loved. Every moment of such loving will nourish you in return. Especially, cherish your own gifts and capacities.
- *Choose and act.* Choose one of your gifts, your possibilities, or your interests. One that you like. Begin to pursue it.

A friend of mine, the mother of four, was getting arthritis. The doctor warned her that it would only get worse. But she was also fascinated by Indian pottery. She had read a little about it. Then she learned that the steps in pottery making that fascinated her most were the un-written secrets. She began to search for them. She learned to make ordinary pottery. Then she went out into the desert and learned to recognize clay and dig it. She tried the Indian methods she knew. She got a small kiln for her experiments. Gradually, over a few years, she followed more and more wherever her fascination led her. Today she is sought after as a teacher of pottery, one who knows some of the ancient secrets. And the arthritis gives her no pain. She began by ignoring her arthritic hands and the doctor's predictions. She only followed her fascination. You can follow her example, even if at first you can give your new love only fifteen minutes a day. *Every* day.

———

Two especially warm capacities are growing within me, which I can trace directly to these steps. The first is that I now can enjoy, even revel in my own gifts. They bring me joy and confidence, so that I rarely recall my limitations. Self-pity has fled, chased away by the sheer delight of living, guided by my God-given abilities.

Second, the gifts of other people bring me joy. It used to be that when I looked at the developed capacities of other lives, I felt stuck, small, useless, and sad about myself. No more. Now I take free, fascinated pleasure in the gifts in other people's lives. My life is richer because of their gifts as well as my own. Yours can be richer, too, and probably richer than mine. Rejoice!

## Suggestions for Prayer

Rejoice and give thanks! You are magnificently blessed by God. With each new blessing you discover, praise, and thank God with all your heart. Honor God in prayer because of the beauty developing outside of prayer. Make that development itself a prayer to God's love. Offer to God the capacities and powers you enjoy the most. Complete them, fulfill them, and give them back to God in joy.

## Scripture Suggestions

*Psalm 37:3-4*
Trust in the LORD, and do good;
   so you will live in the land, and enjoy security.
Take delight in the LORD,
   and he will give you the desires of your heart.

*Proverbs 16:3,20*
Commit your work to the LORD,
   and your plans will be established.

Those who are attentive to a matter will prosper,
   and happy are those who trust in the LORD.

*Luke 10:20*
Nevertheless, do not rejoice at this, that the spirits submit
to you, but rejoice that your names are written in heaven.

*Ephesians 1:3-8*
Blessed be the God and Father of our Lord Jesus Christ,
who has blessed us in Christ with every spiritual blessing
in the heavenly places, just as he chose us in Christ before
the foundation of the world to be holy and blameless before him in love. He destined us for adoption as his children through Jesus Christ, according to the good pleasure
of his will, to the praise of his glorious grace that he freely
bestowed on us in the Beloved. In him we have redemption
through his blood, the forgiveness of our trespasses, according to the riches of his grace that he lavished on us.

*Romans 5:1-4*

Therefore, since we are justified by faith, we have peace with God through our Lord Jesus Christ, through whom we have obtained access to this grace in which we stand; and we boast in our hope of sharing the glory of God. And not only that, but we also boast in our sufferings, knowing that suffering produces endurance, and endurance produces character, and character produces hope.…

Here are some other Scripture references for your reflection:

| | | |
|---|---|---|
| *Psalm 34:1-11* | *Philippians 1:3-6* | *Philippians 3:1* |
| *Psalm 40:1-9* | *Romans 12:9-21* | *John 14:1-4* |
| *Matthew 25:14-30* | *2 Corinthians 9:6-10* | *John 15:1-7* |

## For Reflection

One of the most difficult things you can do is reflect on your own shortcomings and strengths. Take time to reflect and list your limitations and gifts.

- As you feel ready, share these lists with a trusted friend.
- Choose one limitation and one gift to offer especially to God as part of your prayer.

*C*HAPTER *T*EN

# CHOOSE QUALITY RELATIONSHIPS

*The highest form of wisdom is kindness.*
THE TALMUD

*It's only through our relations with others that we develop*
*the outlook of hardiness and come to believe in our own*
*capabilities and inner goodness.*
JOAN BORYSENKO

Central to the life experience of women is our experience of relationships. Here I do not intend just the
relationship with a spouse, but all relationships—children,
friends, extended family, less intense acquaintances—all
these form the fabric of our daily life.

In America, relationships with others are sometimes assumed to be more important than the relationship with
oneself. Yet this book has shown that what is within us
projects outward and creates much of our experience. This

is true not only because we ourselves determine the quality of any experience, but also because people respond to what we are. They respond to the qualities they feel in us and the actions they see.

It has been said often enough: we cannot change others. If we change ourselves, others will change in response. This is the key to understanding how our choices will affect our relationships. What we are, in attitude, feeling, and behavior, will always determine at least fifty percent of the quality of a given relationship. If we change ourselves, the relationship will change to the same extent. We need never be victims of our relationships. We hold a position of considerable power to choose the quality we want in any relationship.

Many women—especially in relationships with men—tend to give away to others all their power to affect the quality of their relationships. They keep hoping that the other person will one day suddenly "see the light" and begin to change, so that the relationship can be more comfortable, more fulfilling, happier for them both.

One hears oneself saying repeatedly, "If only he would..." The assumption is that if the other person would change, everything would be fine. This pattern is an avoidance of emotional responsibility.

The "other person" probably will never change unless there is a compelling reason. A look at our own reluctance to change will tell us why! It is far better to assume that the other person will never change. Then the choices become much more clear.

More deeply, the assumption that the other person should change implies throwing away personal power and responsibility. Even if the other person *did* change, we women would still not have accepted the strength and influence that is truly ours in any relationship. That would mean that our part of the relationship is still weak and still based on a victim-position.

Such a position is unhealthy. It is also unrealistic. We *do* have the capacity to create the quality we want in our relationships. We do it by tending to ourselves. We take responsibility for the relationship's ongoing quality. We make the necessary choices and follow up with the necessary actions. Then—and only then—everything in the relationship is experienced differently. Then it *becomes* different in a healthy and real way.

Will this be easy? Probably not. Changing oneself is seldom easy. Expressing those changes in a relationship that is partly built on the way people "have always been" is even more difficult. Change is possible, however. It is always possible.

Accepting emotional responsibility in a relationship means, simply, that I am responsible for my feelings, no matter what the other person does or says. Many women have difficulty accepting this, even as an idea. Nevertheless, it is true. Acting on it brings great results.

In reality, no one *makes* us feel anything. We do feel or choose to feel in response to what someone else does. We *must* recognize that we have options about our own responses. Our emotional habits are not unconquerable. The question for us, as responsible participants in a relationship, is this: "How shall I feel in response to…?"

For example, my dear husband has a habit of moving or changing things that I have put in a particular place. His reasons are always good ones—to him. But we are different people and we think differently about most things, so his reasons seldom make sense to me. For the first several dozen times he did this, I got insulted ("Doesn't he think I know what I'm doing?") and irritated. Then a day came when he did the same old thing, but I was feeling so grounded and free that morning that it amused me. Then I saw what I'd been doing all along—letting a response from childhood dominate my adult experience.

That was the end of that! In my ongoing amusement, I smilingly said to him when he did it again, "That is sure a strange habit you have, thinking you can read my mind! When you second-guess me like that, you must wonder how I lived without you for so many years! It amuses me— or makes me mad—*depending on the emotional shape I'm in at the time.*" And I grinned at myself and at him too. When he understood I wasn't going to blame him, he laughed at himself and agreed that I usually did have *my own variety* of reasons for what I did.

Many relationships are undermined by tiny, daily events badly handled. It is not the big things, often, but the grinding little things that we misinterpret, re-interpret and allow to erode our love.

We need to be able to distinguish between what is "mine" and what belongs to others. When we sort it out, we can accept responsibility to choose about our own part and let the other part be. We then discover that when fifty percent (our part) of the interaction is altered for the better, the whole interaction changes. In my example, John's small action was his silliness, but my irritation was mine. When I let go of my irritation, he easily saw his own silliness and we grew closer in our shared amusement.

Here is another daily way to practice responsibility with a spouse (I doubt it works with children): the one who is upset by something is the one who fixes it, no matter how it got that way. When the house gets cluttered, the one who cleans up is the one who can't stand it any longer—with *no* blame or inner complaints. I'm responsible for what irritates me.

Someone may object, "But then I'd be doing all the housework!" Well, to whom is it a significant matter? To you? Then it *is* your responsibility.

This habit of self-responsibility eliminates the endless nagging that is so easy to fall into—and that destroys a comforting relationship. Another habit a responsible woman needs to develop is the willingness to ask for what she needs. Somehow, many of us have a romantic notion that our spouses are mind-readers and they will always understand us so easily that they know what we need and what we want. Wrong! They don't and they won't. Furthermore, they are not responsible to "make" us happy. We are responsible to see that our needs are met. That can only happen if we learn to ask for what we want.

It may not be as romantic as the notion of the mind-reading husband (we all want to be surprised by just the right gift at just the right moment, yes?), but it works much better for real relationships. Furthermore, it lasts. It is solid and strong.

Most spouses are willing to give what is needed if they know what it is. Our needs are our responsibility. If we accept this, we ask. Then we accept the response as gift and rejoice in it. The wine of romantic imagination is not nearly as nourishing as the daily bread of responses to our expressed needs and wants.

If asking for what we want is a brand new practice, it would be good to explain it to our partner. Especially important is the mutual understanding that a request is not a demand. It is also likely that sometimes when we ask, we will not receive. But we are not babies—we can wait and we can share our feelings as *our own* feelings—so that communication gradually becomes clearer. Understanding will also increase.

In relationships, the personal decision to take responsibility and to choose what we want implies another basic principle: we decide what qualities we want to experience in the relationship and then we give every effort to putting those qualities into it. Taking responsibility is not about the other person; it is always and only about oneself and one's own choices.

Our choice to change ourselves is ours alone. Our own self is the one area of life in which our power to choose and to create is totally ours. If we don't take our power to choose in both hands and use it, we can be certain our life will go forward on automatic pilot, at the constant mercy of other people's agendas. If we do exercise our power to choose the qualities we desire, not only will our own experience improve, but so will the world around us. Our relationships will also improve.

In many marriages, taking responsibility for personal choice is one of the hardest tasks for women. This seems especially true when the woman wants to grow psychologically or spiritually. Women too often prefer to wait for their husbands to take the lead. As one very intelligent and sincere woman said to me recently, "It would be so nice to share it with my husband." Of course it would! But that decision is *his,* not hers. Are we going to put our emotional growth or our life with God on hold until our spouse "gets it"? If so, we have chosen irresponsibility to ourselves and to God.

Let's assume we want to choose and create the qualities we desire in our relationships, as well as in ourselves. Another question arises: can I convince my husband that he should go this way too?

My answer is: forget it! Our choices are our own. They are about ourselves. Our husbands (or children or friends) may not be interested in our interests, may not be ready for what attracts us. *Each of them has a life to live.* Just as we don't want them to live our lives for us, so we choose to respect them and let them live their lives. We support them with our respect and love.

Too many women have soured their husbands on spiritual matters, not so much by involving themselves, but by insisting on sharing everything with their husbands, usually implying they should have the same interests. In matters religious it is all too easy to be self-righteous about it: "I know this is what God wants, therefore my husband *should* do it too." This violates another person's capacity for choice.

To push the partner to change worsens the relationship immeasurably. It suggests that the other is not good enough as he is. It amounts to saying that the other is not worthy of our love—and that is always an untruth.

When we choose to change ourselves, especially if these changes have to do with spiritual aspirations, we must be attentive to the deepest spiritual principle: love. We must find ways to love the other person more, even as we are changing ourselves.

If loving has always meant a chronic capitulation to the spouse's wishes, the changing of oneself may spawn some surprise and conflict. If help is needed to learn how to be oneself in spite of another person's objections, then get the help. Plenty of counselors are available today to help with self-assertiveness. Learn what you have to learn, but don't abandon respectful love.

So the first attitude to explore and cultivate if you wish to change yourself in the context of your relationships is an honest respect for the other person and a willingness to love him (or her).

Easy? Seldom, if ever. Worth the effort? Always.

We can begin by reminding ourselves that just as we are loved by God, so is the other person. Just as we bear within our souls the image of God, so does the other person. We need to consider well whether we want to violate the sacredness of this person. Will we choose the true spiritual principle of love and respect? Nothing in our own growth will require a violation of the other. Our own growth will require refusal to give away our own power of choice. Sometimes the line can be a fine one. When it is, we need to pray a lot and be willing to discover a way that is good for both ourselves and our spouse.

If we are choosing to become more responsible, we may bewilder our partner with the newness of our choices. But if we act with love and share with great care, we can provide a safety for our partner that will, in the end, give us more space without taking space away from our spouse.

We need to be attentive to our partner's genuine capacities and personal needs. We can explore and define our own boundaries, *for ourselves,* while tending with love to the other.

Here is another example from my own life. There was a time when my spiritual life required deep changes in my understanding and some of my activities. Until then, my husband and I had seen "eye-to-eye" on most of these things. I was about to choose something that I knew might seem pretty weird to him. My choices were not directly about the relationship itself. That was good and loving and gentle. I didn't want to do anything to drive a wedge between us, but I needed to find my own way as well. What to do?

I found that the following aspects were important:

First, I nurtured the relationship, more than before, in

ways that were true to myself. Listening more, giving more freely when it was honest, making sure needs got a response in action, expressing more affection, were some of the aspects I attended to. These actions were not difficult because they were all true expressions of my love for him. I only paid more attention to avoid taking my husband's preferences in the relationship for granted.

Second, I did what I had to do for myself. I did it alone. When time was demanded for my new choices, I tried to keep a balance between my needs and the time we had to share. I did not abandon my work responsibilities, including household tasks. My duties remained and doing them well became part of my new spiritual goals. In all this, however, I made sure that my new practices received the necessary attention. This meant that I got up much earlier, before my husband, and that I sometimes was away in the evening, by myself.

Third, I shared my new efforts and understandings very cautiously, very gradually, and always made sure he understood that these were *my* interests. Nothing new was being required of him, even in my thoughts. As time went on we both saw that the relationship became richer and better as I became more and more my own person spiritually. Then we both relaxed around the changes.

After some years, I see that my growth has inspired his growth, though his takes different forms from mine. Most surprisingly, he has been heard to defend my positions in public—and vociferously! Isn't that delightful? God has so caringly watched over us both and led each of us in the way that we are able to go.

Now, let's review the choices considered in earlier chapters of this book, to explore their possible effects in relationships.

What about pain? If we are in pain and doing nothing with it attitudinally, the chances are we will complain. Probably a lot. How does this affect a relationship? No one likes to live with a complainer. No one will go out to lunch too often with a chronic complainer—unless it's a mutual complaint session!

When complaints about pain are subtracted from relationships, we have more energy for loving our spouse, our child, our friend. When we have come to terms with our own pain in a responsible way, we may sometimes share it with others, but the pain does not dominate our conversations. Our focus can be on loving the other person. Then the relationship deepens.

So we discover that pain need not be poison to our lives. It is an experience that we must deal with by good choices, but then we can get on with our lives, doing what we like, loving those we love.

A friend and I were talking one day about suffering. He was about twenty-five years old when he learned that his father had been suffering with painful physical problems for a number of years. He was astonished because he had experienced his father only as a loving and happy man. With shock, he realized that all the time his father had been so giving, he had been in almost constant pain. In distress, the son cried out to his father, "Why didn't you tell me?"

Quietly, his father replied, "This is *my* pain, given to me. It does not belong to you."

The point is worth pondering.

What about our choices regarding fear?

Fear, among other undesirable results, tends to make us want to cling. Now sometimes we genuinely need momentary comfort and then it is fine to ask for it. Other times, we can choose to deal with our fears ourselves and not burden our relationships with them. If our fears have been chronic and if we have clung dependently to spouses, then we may wish to disengage that clinging and grow up, learning to carry our own fears.

As I mentioned in an earlier chapter, certain kinds of social situations have always terrified me. A few years ago, when I still had to choose self-responsibility consciously, suddenly I was left to my own devices among people who all seemed to know each other. I didn't know what to do. I knew no one. Fear gripped me in much the old way. My husband was present, but he was happily occupied with other people.

My choice: to make him responsible to help me with the fear or to handle it myself, with my own powers. I chose to handle the fear myself. I told my husband that I was going to the car and he could meet me there when he was ready. By the time I got to the car, I was rigid with unnamable fears, but I sat there. When John came, I described my terror, making it clear that it was not about him. It was my own.

When we got home, I went off by myself for a little while. Then it occurred to me that he might like to help if I didn't demand and if I could tell him what would be helpful. So I asked if he would sit with me on the sofa and just hold me until my emotions subsided. He was glad for something to do—and his arms felt wonderful.

And so I learned: as long as I do not make him responsible for my fears, he will help, if he knows what to do.

Of course, as fear continues to diminish its hold on my life, all relationships improve. As I am more free, people like me better and I enjoy them with less and less expectation. More and more, we become cohumans, God's children together, more loving and less defensive.

Anger is the next area in which we make crucial choices. If we are learning that anger is our own, and no longer blaming others for "making us mad," we will already be experiencing the improved quality of our relationships.

If we are not spewing anger, we will be far better partners in any undertaking, from marriage to parenting to neighboring. If we free our corner of the world from our anger, by choosing not to keep it, then to that extent resentment and hatred are dissolved. Love can grow more easily.

What about feelings of unworthiness? If we lack self-respect, we are not able to be equal partners in relationships. We will not carry our share of the relationship well if we are undermined by inferiority feelings.

Feelings of unworthiness can keep us from true loving. The ability to love is the ability to face yourself with honest respect. *Love is not need.* Unworthiness leaves us needy, and we necessarily then project that into our marriages, our parenting, our friendships. Self-respect, on the other hand, enables us to respect and enjoy our family and friends. It enables us to love them without conditions—the only kind of love that will keep them close to us forever.

Guilt has much the same effect in relationships as unworthiness does. Feelings of guilt and inferiority often go together. The chronically guilt-ridden will find it difficult not to demand constant reassurance from a spouse or a child.

Self-respect in relationships is greatly increased when we respond to our guilt feelings as suggested in Chapter Six. When we see them, choose against them, and accept forgiveness, we open our hearts to genuine companionship.

When we do not feel guilty, we are likely to be much less critical of others. Finding fault hurts relationships. If we wish to stop finding fault, dealing with our guilt will certainly help. If we don't feel guilty, but grateful instead, we will not feel critical, but appreciative. What spouse, what friend, doesn't enjoy appreciation? What relationship can thrive without it?

If we participate in good relationships, it is likely that loneliness will not be as constant as if we have none. Still, chronic loneliness can happen. When it does, it infects relationships with an unfillable need. We become bottomless pits into which our family and friends could throw themselves twenty-four hours a day and never fill us. So it is important to our relationships that we choose to do those things for ourselves that will make lonely feelings occasional rather than chronic.

Expectations? Expectations of the other person are deadly in relationships, especially in marriage and with children or toward parents. Our expectations of others bind them. They must be defensive against us if they are to maintain their personal integrity. That is no good.

If we want our relationships to feel free (to us as well as others), we will drop expectations. Just drop them. Our heart can adopt a new attitude: "I set you free of all my past expectations."

Then we can practice daily looking at our spouse with fresh eyes: "I wonder what he will be like today? What charm can I find in him today?"

When we really ponder it, it's not a pleasure to have another person in bondage to us. So—practice letting go of those expectations. Not only will disappointments vanish, but new adventures will open in the relationship. There will even be room for surprises. They will keep the relationship interesting for many more years!

Chapter Nine in this book can be used as a guide to your part in every relationship. Take the steps outlined there. Use them as a lens through which to focus on the limitations and gifts *you* bring to your relationships. You will discover new avenues for self-expression. You will experience your part of the relationship differently. So the whole relationship will shift in quality.

People do not always like change. Some spouses do not like their spouses to change. But if the participants in any relationship are willing to be patient and mutually helpful through times of change, wonders can happen. You can grow into mature relationships as you yourself grow. Mature relationships are more rewarding, more fulfilling than almost anything else on this earth. They are worth far more than the effort required to develop them.

Here, then, are steps you can take to survey the quality of your relationships and to help you discover the choices you want to make. Remember, the power to choose is yours.

- *Take a good look at your feelings about two or three of your most significant relationships.* Are they what you'd like them to be? If not, what is *your* part in your experience of them? (Remember, this is about you, not about the other one.)
- *Choose what qualities you would enjoy in your relationships.* Imagine ways you might express yourself to bring these qualities into your relational experiences.
- *Keep this project to yourself.* Secrecy is power here.
- *Monitor yourself.* See that you do not wait for the other person to change and that you do not crusade for changes in the other person.
- *Ask yourself over and over: "Am I making and acting on responsible choices in this interaction?"*
- *Set the other person free to be himself/herself.*
- *Choose to be your own person first.*
- *Choose respect. Choose love.*

## Suggestions for Prayer

When we are focusing our choices on relationships, it is vital that we pray to see ourselves clearly. It is equally important to consult God about all our choices. We can never fully know another person. God will guide us with the insight we need when we ask and listen sincerely.

Then, too, we need to pray for our partners in relationship. The more we pray for another, the more easily we will love, the less we will want to foist our own inadequacies or expectations onto the other.

When we pray for our partners, let us pray for *God's* way with them. Let our own wishes drop away. Especially we do not pray for the partner to change. We pray instead for the partner to experience love, to discover joy, to feel peaceful, to be fulfilled deep inside.

We may pray for a person to grow, but we must watch ourselves so that we do not dictate the nature of this growth. If we can't keep our mental hands out of the partner's life, then we'd better pray more generally for his or her welfare until we are more healthy.

It is also good to pray that the relationship serve the purposes God has in mind for us, both ourselves and the others. This will help keep us honest and humble—both great virtues in relationships!

## Scripture Suggestions

*Sirach 4:20-28*
Watch for the opportune time, and beware of evil,
    and do not be ashamed to be yourself.

For there is a shame that leads to sin,
and there is a shame that is glory and favor.
Do not show partiality, to your own harm,
or deference, to your downfall.
Do not refrain from speaking at the proper moment,
and do not hide your wisdom.
For wisdom becomes known through speech,
and education through the words of the tongue.
Never speak against the truth,
but be ashamed for your ignorance.
Do not be ashamed to confess your sins,
and do not try to stop the current of a river.
Do not subject yourself to a fool,
or show partiality to a ruler.
Fight to the death for truth,
and the Lord God will fight for you.

*Romans 14:13*
Let us therefore no longer pass judgment on one another, but resolve instead never to put a stumbling block or hindrance in the way of another.

*Ephesians 4:25-32*
So then, putting away falsehood, let all of us speak the truth to our neighbors, for we are members of one another. Be angry but do not sin; do not let the sun go down on your anger, and do not make room for the devil. Thieves must give up stealing; rather let them labor and work honestly with their own hands, so as to have something to share with the needy. Let no evil talk come out of your mouths, but only what is useful for building up, as there is need, so that your words may give grace to those who hear. And do not grieve the Holy Spirit of God, with which you were

marked with a seal for the day of redemption. Put away from you all bitterness and wrath and anger and wrangling and slander, together with all malice, and be kind to one another, tenderhearted, forgiving one another, as God in Christ has forgiven you.

*James 4:11*
Do not speak evil against one another, brothers and sisters. Whoever speaks evil against another or judges another, speaks evil against the law and judges the law; but if you judge the law, you are not a doer of the law but a judge.

Other Scripture references for reflection are as follows:

| | | |
|---|---|---|
| *Sirach 6:5-17* | *Romans 14:13* | *James 3:2-12* |
| *Ecclesiastes 3:1-8* | *1 Corinthians 12:1-26* | *James 5:7-9* |
| *Proverbs 31:10-31* | *Philippians 4:4-91* | *John 4:12-16* |
| *Matthew 10:37* | *1 John 4:19-21* | *James 1:19-21* |

## For Reflection

If you are making efforts toward self-change by choice, you may find yourself in need of sharing with others who will support your choices. This is especially true if those closest to you are uneasy with your new directions.

Reflect individually about these topics, sharing with a trusted other if the need arises:

- What qualities do I want to experience in all my relationships?
- What are some choices I can make and actions I can take to inject these qualities into my relationships?

- Am I being true to myself?
- Am I experiencing love for those affected by my choices?
- What are my fears about relationships if I change?
- How can I best handle these fears?
- Do I respect myself in this process? Do I respect others equally?
- Is my situation too challenging for me to handle alone? Do I need professional help?
- Am I keeping a balance between change and love?

# CHAPTER ELEVEN

# KNOW WHAT
YOU LOVE

*I may not always know my purpose,*
*but it will be clear to me when I need to know.*
*I will behave just as I am supposed to at that moment.*
VICKI SEARS

*Nothing contributes so much to tranquilizing*
*the mind as a steady purpose—a point on which*
*the soul may fix its intellectual eye.*
MARY WOLLSTONECRAFT SHELLEY

If we are working on ourselves, alone or in the context of relationships, we soon discover that our own values need to be clear to us before anything can be chosen to support those values. In other words, we can't make intelligent choices until we know what we want. Discovering what we want is not always an easy project.

Once in a workshop, we participants were told to make a

list of the six aspects of our lives that were most important to us. We did. Then the leader asked us to write down, beside each item, how much time we had spent on that item in the last three weeks.

It was a revelation. Thinking through my daily life from this perspective, I discovered that the aspects of life that were the most important to me were often the last ones to get any attention—or got the least time and effort. I also learned that I was not alone; I was in the majority! Most people—and certainly most women—live whipped about by the winds of circumstances and other people's visions and demands.

How about you?

So the first step toward creating a life that expresses our most dearly held values is to discover what those values are. What do we love the most? What do we want the most? What is the most important to us?

This discovery is easier if we are aware of an overall purpose for our lives. This, for some women, is a first step toward understanding what they want.

Do you know what your purpose in life is? This question does *not* mean, "Do you know what God's purpose for you is?" This question asks about *your* purpose, your aim for your life. (It may comfort some of you to learn that what we want most deeply for ourselves is almost always what God wants *for* us. Does that seem too good to be believed?)

Many women feel something like this: "Oh, I do things— take care of the kids, tend to the household, love my husband, go to church, volunteer in the community. But they are just things that seem to be there. I don't know a specific purpose for my life."

Yet underlying all the many roles a woman plays, usually there is a guiding purpose or leading principle which her life expresses. It often has to do with quality or the values she actually cherishes. She may never have put this guiding purpose into words. Being quite natural to her feelings, her real purpose might seem too ordinary to her. If she did put it into words, she might say something like, "Through all the stress of living, I want to help other people feel important." Or "Even when I'm most busy, I want to remember God." Or "My purpose always is to foster the happiness of my family, then of those I meet."

Usually this purpose is something already known which must only be discovered and expressed consciously. I wasn't so sure about my own purpose in life when I first looked at this question. I felt scattered because I seemed to be wearing so many hats. So I tried to find an underlying theme in all my activities, or most of them. It was rather like looking for the "bottom-line feeling," as outlined in Chapter One.

Eventually, I saw that my purpose in life is threefold: to live ever closer to God, to practice love and peace in all relationships and situations, and to serve by facilitating growth and healing in myself and in others.

Those together are my aim. Those words express in summary form my most cherished values. Before I put those words together and heard my heart's "yes!" to them, I often felt as if I were living by Braille, muddling my way through decisions without a clear vision.

Sometimes a person's aim takes a very concrete form, such as being a champion skater or a concert violinist. I always rather envied those people because for years my own purposes seemed so vague compared to my picture of their purposes. Then I realized that God gives every person a purpose.

When I looked carefully at the purpose I'd discovered, I knew I loved it. I wouldn't trade it for anyone else's, even if

I could. It would be like trying to split my heart in two if I were to abandon the purpose God had already written in my being. That's how I knew that our own purpose is discovered, it is not invented.

Once we are clear about our purpose, we can begin to organize our life and our choices around that purpose. This, too, is a step-by-step process.

Begin by thinking through your purpose and making notes to yourself about it. Try writing out your purpose several times. Re-write it until it suits you just right. Don't share it with anyone else until you are satisfied with it. After all, this is *your* purpose and no one else's. You don't need input from others about this. It is already written in your bones.

The next step is to name the values or principles or processes we already know that support our purpose. In my own case, for example, I knew right away that daily prayer would support my purpose. Certain learning or training would support my purpose. My own good health would support my purpose. Good relationships were the field in which my purpose could be exercised. I saw, too, that certain attitudes supported my purpose. Faith, personal responsibility for my experience, willingness to make my own choices, openness to growth and change, humility before my weaknesses and mistakes—these were all attitudes that would help me express my purpose in the world.

What values support your purpose? What attitudes would support your purpose?

The next step is to get acquainted with how you are living now in relation to your purpose. This means examining how you *actually* spend your time. One way to do that is to keep an hourly log for two or three weeks, so that a clear pattern of where your time goes emerges. Then you can take that log and investigate which of your activities have supported your purpose in these weeks.

When you have a clear statement of purpose and a clear view of how you currently live, you can take the next step: make a list of everything you can think of that you might do to bring your purpose to fulfillment.

For example, when I realized that facilitating healing was part of my aim in life, I also saw that I didn't know anything about it. It was just a strong impulse in my heart. My list of possible actions included reading books on healing of several kinds, talking with people in healing work, taking courses in related subjects, going back to school, praying for guidance and opportunities, being willing to practice what little I already knew—and doing it. 1 was surprised at how many steps I could take. And each step I actually took opened up more possibilities. Eventually, large decisions arose out of all this investigation.

You may know a lot more concretely than I did what you can do to fulfill your aim. You may not need to do all the investigation that I needed. Your list might be such that when you have completed each step you have arrived at your aim. That's wonderful. Each person's process will be a little different.

This process is always based on three main steps, however: knowing your aim, knowing how you are living now, and taking action to bring your aim to reality.

In the process, we need to observe how we make decisions and decide if we want to keep doing it the same way. I had learned, as a child, to clear away all the small stuff before I began on the things I loved and really wanted to do. It was years before I realized that this pattern was backwards. That which I love, that which is most important to me should have top priority in my time and efforts. Then, as I can, I take care of the rest.

For example, when I lived alone, it seemed I was forever trying to clear away clutter that I had created the day before and for which I felt guilty. When I realized how much time and emotional energy was frittered away on this issue, I simply put housework at the bottom of my priority list. There it has stayed. A sparkling, artistically kept house does not support my purpose in life. (Neither would a dirty house, though, so it does eventually get de-cluttered and cleaned.)

The daily decisions (What do I do now? How much time shall I spend on this? Shall I do this or that?) can be made freely according to our aim and the principles which support it.

If you like scheduling (a good idea if many things go on at once in your life), then plan your schedule around those things which are genuinely most important to you, which give your purpose the most possibility for expression. Give your best hours in the day to your purpose, your own special aim. Let the lesser, but necessary, things wait for the time when your energies are less. Give more time to the needs of your aim than to the trivialities that can sometimes be so alluring.

Your pattern will be different from mine. Take the time to see your own pattern. Honor it. Keep what helps you and rearrange or discard what does not help you express your own purpose in life.

Always remember that a healthy you, physically and emotionally, is necessary for the fulfillment of *any* aim in life. Be sure that you include activities that support your health and overall well-being. Recreation, too, must have a place to keep you balanced. By experimentation, you will learn how much time you need for exercise, play, work, creativity, and so on. Spiritual well-being should be included. Prayer certainly nourishes that. Include it, too, and take time for other solitary spiritual practices as you desire them.

There are periods in every woman's life when the demands of family, community, church or friends seem to take up every minute of available time and every ounce of energy. "Seem to" is accurate since this situation is seldom totally the case. We feel torn in too many directions, oftentimes, because we have not claimed any time for our own direction. When we are out of touch with our own values, we easily allow ourselves to be overwhelmed by needs of others. In reality, no one needs to have everything they want all the time—not children, not teens, not spouse, and not ourselves. We women are the ones who must be willing to set limits and make fair distributions of our own energies and attention. That is a task no one can do for us.

One woman I know did it the simplest possible way. She announced to her family that she was going to try an experiment. Each person was going to get a certain number of hours a week from her and they could decide what they wanted to do with those hours. She decided the number for each person. (Her husband got the most.) To her astonishment, after a few missteps, everybody enjoyed deciding what was most important between her and them. When their time was up, they knew they had to wait until next week.

The most astounding result to her was that after a few weeks of this rather arbitrary experiment, all of them developed a new respect for her and for their time with her. She no longer had to limit everybody, because they began asking her if she had time and energy to give them. And for the first time in years, her husband no longer felt cheated by the time she gave to the children.

Of course, included in this time-for-everybody plan was daily time for herself as well. That was what really made the plan work. During her time for herself, her choices supported her stated purpose in life. Except for real emergencies, she expressed her most important values for living every single day in some way, even if small. "Finally," she said to me, "I feel as if I have my own soul."

Experiment. When you know where you want to go, and where you are now, you will discover ways to get there. It's as sure as daylight! And it's a great delight to be exploring and expressing your own life's real reason for being.

So here again are the main steps to creating a life based on the values you cherish:

- *Formulate your own purpose in life.*
- *Explore the principles and attitudes that support your purpose.*
- *Know what you want most and what you value most.*
- *Examine how you are living right now in relation to your purpose, your values, and your deepest desires.*
- *List possible steps that will guide your action as you move to change your life.*
- *Observe your own decision-making process and adjust it to match your purpose in life.*
- *Organize your life around your purpose.*
- *Make necessary adjustments in your responses to other people's demands.*
- *Take some time every day for yourself and attention to your purpose, even if it's only twenty minutes.*
- *Act! Begin now.*

## Suggestions for Prayer

Pray to see clearly your own purpose or aim in life. Pray to see clearly how you are living now. Pray for the insight to discover what to do about what you have found out. Pray for the strength and creativity and determination to do it!

Give thanks to God for giving you such a beautiful purpose. Express your appreciation for God's support as you begin consciously to fulfill your purpose.

## Scripture Suggestions

*Proverbs 25:16*
If you have found honey, eat only enough for you,
   or else, having too much, you will vomit it.

*Sirach 30:14-15*
Better off poor, healthy, and fit
   than rich and afflicted in body.
Health and fitness are better than any gold,
   and a robust body than countless riches.

*Matthew 5:13*
You are the salt of the earth; but if salt has lost its taste, how can its saltiness be restored? It is no longer good for anything, but is thrown out and trampled under foot.

*Matthew 7:1-5*
"Do not judge, so that you may not be judged. For with the judgment you make you will be judged, and the measure you give will be the measure you get. Why do you see the speck in your neighbor's eye, but do not notice the log in your own eye? Or how can you say to your neighbor, 'Let me take the speck out of your eye,' while the log is in your own eye? You hypocrite, first take the log out of your own eye, and then you will see clearly to take the speck out of your neighbor's eye."

*Philippians 3:12*
Not that I have already obtained this or have already reached the goal, but I press on to make it my own, because Christ Jesus has made me his own.

Other possibilities for scriptural reflection are as follows:

| | | |
|---|---|---|
| *Psalm 19:14* | *Proverbs 5:15-17* | *Matthew 13:44-46* |
| *Psalm 25:16* | *Proverbs 16:3* | *Luke 14:28-32* |
| *Psalm 103:1-5* | *Wisdom 9:4-6* | *Ephesians 5:8b-17* |

## For Reflection

It is often most helpful to write down the goals and purposes you have chosen for yourself. You may wish to record the answers to these questions:

- What are my three most significant, bottom-line desires?
- What people, things, events, and so on, are most important to me?
- What are my most basic values?
- What changes would I like to experience in my life?
- What actions could I take to move toward fulfillment of my purpose?
- What one step will I take *this week* to fulfill my purpose?
- What could I do every day to promote my own aim?

# Chapter Twelve

# Make a Choice
# for God's Kingdom

*There is a divine plan of good at work in my life.*
*I will let go and let it unfold.*
RUTH P. FREEDMAN

*The world cannot be discovered by a journey of miles...*
*only by a spiritual journey...by which we arrive*
*at the ground at our feet, and learn to be at home.*
WENDELL BERRY

This book has emphasized the power we have to choose our own attitudes and our own actions. This power enables us to create the life we want, to allow negative attitudes to die away and new ones to grow strong and mature. This power of the will is the core of a beautiful life if we choose to put it to work for us.

If you have been experimenting as you read, you will have already made wonderful discoveries about the power of your own choice, especially about your attitudes and emotions. The principles here are true. They give a much finer quality to all of your experience. The principles do work. When put into practice, these principles do change lives, as I have learned from my own experience.

One aspect of our living bears a somewhat different relationship to our power of choice than anything we've discussed so far. That is our spiritual life, our relationship with God.

In our relationship with God, our capacity for personal choice gradually becomes subordinated to our potential for responding consistently to God's guidance in our hearts. When we want to live ever closer to God, our vision of our own life-experience changes. Some things that seemed vital before no longer seem so important. Other things that we practically never did or hardly noticed become central to a new approach to our life.

The choices discussed in this book are more about attitudes than circumstances. They imply a life of self-empowerment, self-responsibility. They are highly charged and strong. They are usable in any circumstances (short of major trauma when one may need professional assistance). All of the attitudinal choices in this book are compatible with our growing experience of God. When we choose whatever attitude makes *us* better, we are choosing an inner stance that will open our hearts to more of God's influence.

When we want a profound relationship with God, however, choices and our relationship to choice in general will shift.

First, we will be invited—as all Christians are—to make a fundamental choice and to subordinate everything to that single choice. I am still learning about how this works in living, but I'm happy to share what I know so far.

We begin with Jesus' words in Matthew 6:25-33. The fundamental choice to be made is whether or not we want to put the kingdom first.

To make that choice, we need to understand that the Kingdom (or the reign) of God, as Jesus understood it, is primarily a way of living right now, a quality of life that depends on intimate and ever-deepening union with the Lord in this our familiar, daily life. It happens inside us first (just as everything else we've been considering does) and then expresses itself in our circumstances, our relationships, our work—everything in our life. The Kingdom of God is always within us first. If it does not come alive within us, it cannot welcome us elsewhere—not even in heaven.

If we choose to put Jesus and the Kingdom first, how can we begin? We begin by acknowledging that we do want to put God first. In actuality we don't know what that means and we don't know how to do it. So we pray. We pray over and over again for the insight and the character to actually give ourselves to this mysterious and wonderful Kingdom of the heart filled with God. When we genuinely want this to be our first and foundational choice, gradually we will be led into discoveries about how it works and what our part is.

One thing is clear: dedication to the Kingdom changes our relationship to the power of choice. After that one choice, all other choices, little by little, step by step, are submitted to God's choices for us. Our attitude becomes that of the willing, grateful receiver more than that of the one who knows how to make things happen. Everything we have learned in our journey this far will be useful, but it will have a different feeling and a fresh, new, unexpected outcome. God is not predictable—but God is always good.

So, relying on God in a new way, our first resolve is to leave the results of all our choices strictly up to God.

We usually make choices, whether of action or of attitude or of purposes and values, based on expected results. We calculate how we think our choices will turn out. We hope things will turn out in certain ways. If we pay attention as our choices fulfill themselves, we know that sometimes they turn out in ways we expect and sometimes they don't.

When we give the results of our choices to God, we no longer choose according to anticipated outcomes. We choose according to what is good, maybe, or what is loving, or the guidance we have received in our heart. We make the best choice we know and then hand it over to God and leave it. Its results will come in God's good time, according to God's will.

At first this may feel as if we're abandoning our personal power all over again. Experience will show, however, that our personal power is set free in a new way.

I have found that giving the results of my choices to God opens up vast possibilities that I hadn't dreamed of. God always has more options than I can imagine, and he doesn't hesitate to create new ones! This has become one of the reasons I enjoy a freelance economic life—it leaves all the doors open for God's abundant responses. God's results sometimes match what I might have figured, but more often they are better, more interesting, more loving, and more fulfilling than my expectations. God's unexpected results always strengthen me in some noticeable way. God is always doing more than one thing at a time for my betterment!

A wonderful side-benefit of leaving the results up to God is protection. More than once, I've made a choice that might have resulted in disaster. But it didn't, because God knew better than I. Even when I have been totally wrong in some choice, it seems that God softens the consequences of my lack of wisdom—*if* I have given the results to God.

What we cling to for ourselves, we get to keep. Sometimes the results aren't so desirable. But when God gives them, they will always be for our highest benefit. God is our greatest benefactor, when we allow God to be.

When we give the results of our choices to the Lord, worry and insecurity are greatly reduced. They may not disappear all at once because worry and insecurity are emotional habits. They have considerable strength and tenacity inside us. As we become more open to God's ways, these habits gradually give way to trust, because we discover in experience that God is totally worthy of our trust.

Gradually we begin to experience a new bottom-line feeling about our life. For many of us, it feels strange because it is so completely new. It is called contentment.

If God is taking over the results of all our choices, then we can relax and let circumstances reveal to us the divine will in our lives. When we finally "get it," that everything comes to us from the loving heart of God, our discontent erodes away. We are left with peaceful hearts. The best part is, a peaceful heart is the place where God himself loves to live.

So, instead of frantically trying to keep control over every aspect of our life, we gradually learn to do something better. We learn to surrender ourselves to what is given to us and what is asked of us.

Spiritual surrender does not mean collapse. It means a deep willingness that God's will should happen in every part of ourselves and our circumstances. Our life gradually is no longer our own. Little by little, we surrender it to God, giving it into loving hands that are far more powerful than our choices ever can be.

I recall the day I suddenly was aware that I wasn't "running my own show" any more. The shift was inwardly palpable. Life didn't *feel* the same anymore. I'd love to be able to say that on that day I gave up all concern for everything and lived without resistance in the flow of the Holy Spirit. So saintly I am not—yet. I am on the way and it's the most exciting journey imaginable.

It does not yet mean that I welcome every circumstance without a moment's resistance. Nor does it mean that I have no desires and make no choices. It does mean that deep down inside I know that my resistances are on the way out, my desires are lessening in intensity, and my choices are fine things to do but not ultimately significant. Only God is ultimately significant.

When I experience resistance, as soon as I see it, I pray to have this hardness of heart dissolved. When a desire grips my mind and emotions—and if I catch it!—I turn it over to God. It sounds like, "This desire has arisen, Lord. My life is becoming yours. I offer this desire to you and surrender now to its results." When I make choices, I do the best I know to do, knowing that the whole thing could be totally changed in a moment.

Someone has asked, "Do you know how to make God laugh?" The answer is, "Tell him your plans." True. So above my complicated wall calendar, I have a sign: *Making God Laugh.* It reminds me that it's my job to do the best I know to do, as much of the time as I can. It's God's job to bring the results—in spite of my calendar!

When those results come, I may or may not remember that they are God's, depending on how spiritually alert I am on that day! But sooner or later I get it—and then I have a "surrender party" and give the whole sequence of prayers and events back to God. And I face whatever has been given.

For example, a year ago it seemed clear to me that a big next step in my life was to become a massage therapist so I could facilitate healing in this way. The training I felt guided toward seemed to require an impossible amount of money for me to earn in the allotted time. My husband (retired) would be home alone for two months. I would have to go to a strange city (three thousand miles away), find housing, use city buses instead of driving daily to school. And an extraordinarily expensive plane fare seemed unavoidable. Yet the guidance I felt toward this training was so strong!

What to do? I chose to say a big, solid "yes" to the training and enrolled in the school. Now the rest was up to God because, although I could plan, I couldn't really see any further. The results were amazing, and different from my imaginings, so I had to surrender to each one as it came along, letting go of my own best plans.

God's summer of training included a cross-country trip by car with my husband—and his solo month-long return trip which he loved; my cross-country return with a friend who needed the second driver; a delightful new friendship with my hostess for half the summer; and half the summer living with one of my dearest friends, who needed company right then. Bonus: we lived two blocks from school and five blocks from the Pacific Ocean! Money affairs were totally re-arranged before the training was over, and I returned home with everything I needed and a bit left over to start a massage practice. In my smartest reckoning, I would never have come up with all that!

Gradually, then, we learn to let our lives unfold more simply, daily, with hearts surrendered to God's desires *for* us. They are always more than enough. We go on choosing, especially our attitudes, but the basic attitude we choose is surrender to God's love. This must be chosen again and again until it stabilizes in our hearts. Of course, we make it more likely for ourselves if we begin by surrendering to the small things that don't challenge us too much. God is infinitely patient, so there's no hurry to get it all right the first time!

As we surrender to what is given, we learn also to surrender to what is asked. There are some jobs I'd rather not do ever again, for example. I'm good at them but I'd like to avoid them. From all indications so far, God does not agree with me. Requests for my work keep coming. Because it is God whom my heart desires, and these assignments come clearly from him (after all, I do nothing to encourage them!), I say yes.

Saying yes to God means giving my very best to what is asked. Slipshod efforts or efforts that do not acknowledge God in the doing or efforts that are not offered to God— these are no longer acceptable.

Surrendering to God's requests means that we become instruments. That's all. Humbling? I suppose. But equally important, it's solid and secure. The tasks are no longer about us. They are God getting something done that he wants done. We are, at best, surrendered servants of divine love.

It's a daily challenge. The results of working at it, however, increase the value of life exponentially. In the surrendered life, there is more freedom than one could otherwise imagine. Credits and blames are reduced, so that equanimity begins to grow in the heart. Equanimity means that eventually we will be able to live in awareness of God every second. What love that will bring!

In the surrendered life, there is more power to create the beautiful and the effective in all our circumstances. Just as I could not design last summer as well as God did, so all other choices and yeses are magnified to everyone's greatest good.

In the surrendered life, gratitude flows like a constant stream, changing with the seasons, but never dry. Joy comes to live in the heart—to stay. Love and peace, too, are more and more permanent residents in our experience.

Isn't all that what we wished for when we began to learn to make our own choices, to create responsibly our own life?

And there is experience of God, the Source of every beauty, every joy, every peaceful moment, and the Spring of all life, all love.

The most astounding realization in the adventure so far is that the surrendered life recognizes all the splendor as pure gift. One does the best one can, but then it is all re-done by the Creator and given to us as if we had never done a thing! For this, we need only an open, increasingly surrendered heart. For such a heart, we practice choosing the highest attitudes we know—and giving the results to the Lord of the universe.


## Suggestions for Prayer

Prayer that supports a surrendered life sounds a little like this:

*What do you want now, Lord?*

*I don't know what to choose, but this is my best guess. Here it Is. Make of it what You want.*

*Okay. I'm not sure this is what I'd have wished, but I'll take it. Thanks for sending it. Please show me how to use it.*

*Wow! That's fabulous, Lord! Thank You so much! Thank you so much! Thank you so much!*

## Scripture Suggestions

*Psalm 34:1-3*
I will bless the LORD at all times;
 his praise shall continually be in my mouth.
My soul makes its boast in the LORD;
 let the humble hear and be glad.
O magnify the LORD with me,
 and let us exalt his name together.

*Psalm 37:3-7*
Trust in the LORD, and do good;
 so you will live in the land, and enjoy security.
Take delight in the LORD,
 and he will give you the desires of your heart.

Commit your way to the LORD;
 trust in him, and he will act.
He will make your vindication shine like the light,
 and the justice of your cause like the noonday.

Be still before the LORD, and wait patiently for him;
 do not fret over those who prosper in their way,
 over those who carry out evil devices.

*Psalm 37:23-24*
Our steps are made firm by the LORD,
 when he delights in our way;
though we stumble, we shall not fall headlong,
 for the LORD holds us by the hand.

*Ecclesiastes 7:13-14*
*Consider the work of God; who can make straight what he has made crooked? In the day of prosperity be joyful, and in the day of adversity consider; God has made the one as well as the other, so that mortals may not find out anything that will come after them.

*Matthew 7:7-11*
"Ask, and it will be given you; search, and you will find; knock, and the door will be opened for you. For everyone who asks receives, and everyone who searches finds, and for everyone who knocks, the door will be opened. Is there anyone among you who, if your child ask for bread, will give a stone? Or if the child asks for a fish, will give a snake? If you then, who are evil, know how to give good gifts to your children, how much more will your Father in heaven give good things to those who ask him!"

*Philippians 1:9-11*
And this is my prayer, that your love may overflow more and more with knowledge and full insight to help you to determine what is best, so that in the day of Christ you may be pure and blameless, having produced the harvest of righteousness that comes through Jesus Christ for the glory and praise of God.

Other Scripture references for reflection include:

| | | |
|---|---|---|
| *2 Samuel 22:21-31* | *Isaiah 55:1-3* | *John 15:1-11* |
| *Psalm 57:8-11* | *Matthew 6:19-34* | *Acts 10:9-16* |
| *Isaiah 40:3-5,28-31* | *Matthew 25:14-30* | *Philippians 4:11-13* |
| *Isaiah 41:13* | *Luke 9:23-25,46-48* | *1 John 3:18-22* |
| *Isaiah 49:15-16* | | |

## For Reflection

Focus on your individual responses to these questions:

- Why do I try to calculate results before choosing action?
- What is my resistance to surrender?
- Why am I not contented?
- Do I want God's Kingdom to be my top priority? Why or why not?